SHIPWRECKS
and
LOST TREASURES
Outer Banks

Legends and Lore, Pirates and More!

BOB BROOKE

ILLUSTRATIONS BY PAUL G. HOFFMAN

The Globe Pequot Press

GUILFORD, CONNECTICUT

I dedicate this book to all those brave souls who lost their lives
in their battle with the sea off the coast of the Outer Banks.

Text design by Lisa Reneson
Illustrations and map border by Paul G. Hoffman
Map by Rusty Nelson © Morris Book Publishing, LLC

Library of Congress Cataloging-in-Publication Data is available.
ISBN: 978-0-7627-4507-4

Manufactured in the United States of America
First Edition/First Printing

To buy books in quantity for corporate use
or incentives, call **(800) 962–0973**
or e-mail **premiums@GlobePequot.com.**

Contents

Contents

Contents

Outer Banks Shipwrecks...

1. *Enterprize* — 1822
2. *William Gibbons* — 1836
3. *Carroll* — 1837
4. *Home* — 1837
5. Steam Packet *Pulaski* — 1838
6. *Orline St. John* — 1854
7. *Pocahontas* — 1862
8. *Nuova Ottavia* — 1876
9. *Huron* — 1877
10. *Metropolis* — 1878
11. *City of Houston* — 1878
12. *M. & E. Henderson* — 1879
13. *Angela* — 1883
14. *Nellie Wadsworth* — 1885
15. *Henry Simmons* — 1889
16. *Strathairly* — 1891
17. *Nathan Esterbrook Jr.* — 1893
18. *Richard S. Spofford* — 1894
19. *E. S. Newman* — 1896
20. *George L. Fessenden* — 1898
21. *Aaron Reppard* — 1899
22. *Virginia* — 1900
23. *Sarah D. J. Rawson* — 1905
24. *Carroll A. Deering* — 1921
25. *Queen Anne's Revenge* — 1718

And Where To Find Them

8 10

15
21
17 2
13 12 20
23 22 1 16
14 3 9
19
24

bemarle Sound

Pamlico Sound

7
6

25
4 18

ATLANTIC OCEAN

N

11
5

Introduction

To many, the Outer Banks, a thin chain of barrier islands running parallel to the mainland of North Carolina, are synonymous with shipwrecks. Stretching nearly 175 miles south from Virginia to Cape Lookout, they're the final resting place for more than one thousand ships that wrecked offshore. This book tells the stories behind twenty-five of those wrecks.

The northernmost island, Currituck Banks, runs from the Virginia border to Bodie Island below Nags Head. Next in the chain is Pea Island, running southward to Cape Hatteras and home to North Carolina's only lifesaving station with an all-black crew. Chicamacomico, one of the original seven lifesaving stations on the Outer Banks built in 1874, stood at the northern end of Kinnakeet Banks, on what is today Hatteras Island.

Of all the places on the Banks, Cape Hatteras is perhaps the most infamous. At the easternmost point of North Carolina, Hatteras looks out over dreaded Diamond Shoals, the heart of what's known as the "Graveyard of the Atlantic." Here, the northward thrust of the warm Gulf Stream and the southward push of the cold Labrador Current collide, creating one of the most unpredictable sea routes on the East Coast of North America. Unstable weather patterns, shallow waters, and shifting sandbars mix in a volatile area that has claimed hundreds of ships and lives.

Because the Gulf Stream flows north at about four miles per hour, it was a problem for sailing vessels heading south. Unless there was a strong tail wind, ships could make little headway against the current. Before the advent of steam engines, vessels traveling south on the Gulf Stream route had little choice but to sail beyond the current, far into the Atlantic Ocean, or to sail down a narrow corridor between the Gulf Stream and the shore of the Outer Banks. Hugging the shore was tricky even in favorable winds and usually deadly when combined with stormy winds and high seas.

Steam powered many oceangoing vessels beginning in the mid-1830s, although most also had sails to provide extra power or in case of engine failure. Though steamships were less at the mercy of contrary winds and the push of the Gulf Stream, they suffered from fires and boiler explosions and could be stranded as easily as sailing ships. Turbulent seas frequently extinguished boiler fires aboard foundering vessels, rendering them helpless.

Throughout the nineteenth and early twentieth centuries, crates, boxes, and barrels of sugar, rum, whisky, gold, and silver, as well as furniture and household goods, continually littered the Banks' beaches and dunes soon after wrecks, along with the bodies of unfortunate passengers and seamen that the sea had claimed. Local residents combed the beaches for anything they could use. And what they couldn't use, they traded to people on the mainland or to passing ships. More and more people came to live on the Banks, drawn by the lure of these treasures, which they assumed were theirs for the taking.

A rash of mid-nineteenth century maritime disasters convinced the U.S. Congress to appropriate funds for government-sponsored lifesaving stations. In 1852, it paid for surfboats to be stationed at Wilmington, Ocracoke, and Bodie Islands, to be placed in the custody of the customs revenue collector. It wasn't until 1871, following another series of shipwrecks, that Congress funded the Revenue Marine Bureau within the U.S. Treasury Department, giving it responsibility over sea rescues. The new legislation authorized seven lifesaving stations to be built on the Outer Banks in 1874 at Jones Hill, Caffeys Inlet, Kitty Hawk, Nags Head, Bodie Island, Chicamacomico, and Little Kinnakeet.

Improvements in ship safety and the passing of the age of sail helped make major shipwrecks a thing of the past by the close of World War I. Fewer wrecks meant the need for fewer lifesavers, so the U.S. Government merged the Lifesaving Service with the coast guard. And while the new organization would continue to rescue wreck survivors, its members would work more to prevent them in the first place.

This book hopes to provide as realistic an account as possible of some of the most interesting natural shipwrecks along the Outer Banks during the nineteenth and early twentieth centuries. Told in short-story style using vivid descriptions and dialogue, these accounts allow readers to relive the harrowing moments as ships' crews and passengers struggled against the power of the sea. It's to all those who lost their lives and now lie at peace in the "Graveyard of the Atlantic" that these stories are dedicated.

SHIPWRECKS
── *and* ──
LOST TREASURES
Outer Banks

1

Horsing Around

ENTERPRIZE—1822

The air had just begun to crisp and the trees showed tinges of orange, rust, and red as fall settled over New England. Men loaded rum, lime, crocks, and lumber into the hold of the schooner *Enterprize*, docked at Bristol, Rhode Island, during the first days of October, 1822. Its passengers, fifteen in all, made themselves at home in the ship's tiny cabins as they readied for their long voyage to Charleston, South Carolina. One of them remained on deck directing the loading of a special piece of cargo, his horse.

At last all was ready and the ship got underway, sailing under a cobalt-blue sky with a stiff but fair wind to her back, billowing her sails and pushing the vessel ahead at full speed.

As the *Enterprize* passed Hampton Roads, Virginia, on October 26, a thick fog settled over the sea. "Steady as she goes," ordered Captain Ephriam Eldridge to his helmsman. The fog continued through the night. Shortly before dawn the next morning, a severe jolt threw the *Enterprize*'s passengers and crew out of their hammocks. The schooner had struck a sand bar. Water poured into the hold. Captain Eldridge knew he was somewhere to the north of Cape Hatteras, but he had no idea where or how far his ship was from shore.

"Everyone into the rigging," he shouted. By this time, the passengers had come up on deck and immediately took to the rigging. The crew followed soon behind as the waves began breaking over the stranded vessel.

"Get down out of the rigging and pump her out," the captain barked to his crew. "She's not breaking up, and we still have a chance to get her off this sand bar." The crewmen scrambled below and began to pump out the hold, but their efforts were fruitless, as the seawater poured in faster than they could pump it out. Suddenly one of them cried, "Fire in the hold!" Somehow the load of lime had caught fire. Now, it seemed the passengers and crew had a choice about how they would die—to drown or be burned to death.

"We must all surely perish," exclaimed passenger William Gardiner. And in an effort to comfort the others, he said, "The Lord is a prayer hearing and a prayer answering God. I cherish the hope that we should escape. Let us pray." Many fell to their knees and prayed—something some had never done.

"What if we push the horse over the side?" suggested one of the passengers. "Perhaps if he can reach land, we can, too." So several passengers went to the horse's pen, led him to the side and gently pushed him overboard. He hit the water with a splash but seemed to be able to right himself and started for shore. Everyone cheered.

The horse had no trouble reaching land since the ship had run aground so close to shore that he could have almost waded in. When the passengers and crew saw that the horse had made

He hit the water with a splash but seemed to be able to right himself and started for shore.

it, they immediately scrambled overboard to follow him and saved themselves.

As the sun moved farther up from the horizon, the tide fell, so some tried to offload some of the cargo. Meanwhile, a few passengers had discovered the wheel tracks of a cart in the sand on the beach. They followed the cart tracks and soon met three men on horseback. "Where are we?" one of the passengers asked.

"You're on Chicamacomico Banks about thirty miles north of Cape Hatteras Lighthouse," one of the men replied. "How did you get here?"

"Our ship, the *Enterprize*, ran aground just offshore," the passenger said, pointing to the stranded vessel.

The men took the survivors to the small village of Chicamacomico to get dry clothes and food. There they made arrangements with Captain Edward Scarborough of Kinnakeet to hire his schooner, the *Thomas A. Blount*, to take them across the sound to Ocracoke. They left the horse that had led them to safety on Chicamacomico Banks. The survivors boarded the *Thomas A. Blount* late the next morning. No one expected any trouble during the short trip, but by mid-afternoon the weather changed and the winds increased. As Captain Scarborough tried to keep his vessel on course, a huge wave washed him overboard, never to be seen again.

The horse that led the passengers and crew of the *Enterprize* to safety was the only one to do so in the history of the Outer Banks.

2

Negligence at Sea

WILLIAM GIBBONS—1836

Steam packet boats began plying the waters along the eastern coast of the United States as early as 1818, offering passenger service between ports. Passengers saw traveling by steamer to be a definite improvement over land travel by stagecoach. Not only was the trip usually smoother and more enjoyable, it took less time. On October 8, 1836, 140 passengers, including thirty-two women and fourteen children, boarded the wooden paddle steamer *William Gibbons* for a trip on its regularly scheduled run between New York and Charleston, South Carolina.

Nothing seemed out of the ordinary, except that the ship had a new captain for this voyage. But just hours before she was ready to set sail, Captain Spinney, her new master, notified the *Gibbons*'s owners that he had taken ill and couldn't make the trip. They immediately called upon E. L. Halsey, the ship's former captain, now retired, to take over. Captain Halsey said he would do it on one condition: He would see to the comfort and care of the passengers if the first mate and navigator could take charge of the ship's navigation. The owners agreed, because steam packets depended on sailing on schedule.

Captain Halsey had made approximately four hundred trips south along North Carolina's coast past Cape Hatteras. He knew the route, and the dangers. For the last two years before his retirement earlier that same year, he had captained the *William Gibbons* on the New York–Charleston run. He decided to call it quits after the *Gibbons*'s steam chimney, next to which he had been standing warming his feet, suddenly exploded, killing three of his crew and two passengers. Such explosions were a common hazard before the invention of the steam pressure valve.

Halsey fully entrusted the operation of the ship to First Mate Joshua Andrews and his navigator, T. W. Winship. The owners had instructed him to assist the passengers, preside at the dinner table, and to offer any advice the first mate might require. Other than that, Halsey had expected this to be a typically quiet and relaxing voyage.

After steaming out of New York Harbor with the tide at 4:00 p.m., Mr. Andrews headed the *William Gibbons* south along the coast, maintaining a steady speed of ten miles an hour. By the following evening, the ship stood off the Outer Banks. Stars twinkled in the night sky, but without a moon, visibility was poor. The last lighthouse before Cape Hatteras stood at Cape Henry, so it was impossible for Mr. Andrews or Mr. Winship to see where they were headed. To compensate, they had the leadsman take soundings every fifteen minutes. "Eleven fathoms, sir," he reported at midnight—just what Winship expected.

At dinner that evening, Captain Halsey sat at the head of the table and chatted amiably with his passengers. Afterward, he retired to the saloon to have a cigar and a glass of port wine with the gentlemen on board. Bidding his good nights, he hastened to the bridge to chat with Mr. Andrews.

By 2:30 a.m., as Halsey was about to make his way down to his cabin, he noticed a light at a distance off the port bow. "That should be Cape Hatteras Light," he said.

"Yes, sir, I believe it is," Andrews agreed. Throughout the following hour, Andrews ordered the leadsman to take soundings. The water depth had increased to fifteen fathoms, then to seventeen, and finally to nineteen.

"I definitely see breakers around Diamond Shoals, sir," said Andrews as he gazed through his spyglass. Halsey took the spyglass to look for himself and agreed.

The leadsman continued to take soundings and an hour and a quarter later reported he couldn't reach bottom.

"I believe we have passed Diamond Shoals, sir," said Andrews told Captain Halsey. "I'm changing course to the west and am heading her for Cape Lookout."

For a while, all went well as the *Gibbons* sailed through the night. The passengers lay asleep in their cabins until suddenly, at 4:40 a.m., the ship bumped into something, throwing many of them onto the floor. Some of the men ran up on deck to see what had happened. In the meantime, the vessel moved abruptly forward before settling down. By this time, Captain Halsey had appeared on deck. "What's going on, Mr. Andrews?" he asked.

"I'm not sure, sir, but I think we've just hit a sand bar," replied the confused first mate.

"How could that be, sir? I thought she was headed toward Cape Lookout."

"I did, but it seems the light we saw wasn't at Cape Hatteras as I had thought."

"Blundering fool," the captain said in disgust. "Reverse engines." Even though Captain Halsey took control of the ship, it was too late; damage had already been done to the rudder. After repeated efforts to back the ship off the shoal, the *Gibbons* ran aground once again.

An hour or so later, the sun began to rise above the horizon. Captain Halsey could see people standing on the shore. "Mr. Andrews, take a boat and row ashore to see if there are accommodations of some sort for our passengers," ordered Halsey.

Andrews took several crewmen and rowed to the beach. "What is this place?" he asked of the bystanders. "And is there a shelter where our passengers might stay until help arrives?"

"This be New Inlet, sir, at the northern end of the Banks," replied one of the bystanders. "There are two deserted houses over yonder about a mile. And Mr. John Midgett has ample provisions at his place about four miles down the beach."

Upon returning to the ship and reporting his findings, Captain Halsey immediately ordered the launching of the *Gibbons's* other boat. Andrews followed the captain's orders, taking six to eight passengers with him at a time. He was only able to remove 116 of them before the wind grew stronger and, in combination with high tide, made the sea rough. The remaining passengers, huddled together on the deck, refused to board the boats.

Meanwhile, those who made it ashore found themselves crammed together in the two small abandoned buildings with very little water. Even though John Midgett had sup-

For a while, all went well as the Gibbons *sailed through the night.*

plies, no one had a way to fetch them. And so they remained for three days.

Back on the ship, the remaining passengers and crew struggled to survive a fierce nor'easter that had blown in. By the morning of Tuesday, October 11, some of the crew had discovered the liquor for the bar and helped themselves. First Mate Andrews joined them. Soon they had rifled through every trunk and bag onboard and had stolen the more valuable items. The firemen also sifted through the mail the *Gibbons* was carrying. Captain Halsey had lost all control of his vessel. All he could do was wait out the storm.

Mr. Andrews and the rest of the drunken crewmen took the other boat and set sail for Elizabeth City, North Carolina, where they tried to sell the jewelry and other valuable items they stole from the passengers. After being arrested, they stood trial in Raleigh. Mr. Andrews received a token fine, which he paid from the money gained from the sale of the stolen goods. The court dismissed the charge against the four firemen.

Meanwhile, Captain Halsey had several crewmen row him and the remaining passengers to shore as soon as the winds had died down. There he arranged passage to Norfolk, Virginia, for the passengers and the remaining crew.

The passengers, who Captain Halsey comforted on the voyage, finally turned against him in the end, accusing him of gross negligence, a charge he overwhelmingly denied. After such a problem-filled voyage, he retired once again and swore he'd never command another ship.

3

Canine to the Rescue

CARROLL—1837

The air was warm but balmy, the sky bright blue on the morning of January 25, 1837, as the crew of the brig *Carroll* made ready for sail with the tide from New Orleans bound for Baltimore, then farther on to Boston. Captain Mitchell saw to the loading of her cargo of hides, pork, lard, cotton, and castor oil as his dog, Pillow, dozed lazily in the sun.

"Good morning, Captain," said a robust man carrying a valise. "I'm one of your passengers, Samuel Bangs."

"Welcome aboard and a fine morning to you, sir," replied the captain as he turned and shook the man's hand. "You there, help Mr. Bangs with his belongings," he ordered one of the crew as two black men carried aboard a heavy trunk. Pillow barked at them and then resumed his nap.

"I've been traveling in Mexico for several months and am looking forward to getting home," said Bangs. "I trust we shall have no problem setting off today?"

"No, sir," replied the captain. "'Tis a good day for sailing."

Leaving New Orleans, the *Carroll* glided down the Mississippi into the Gulf of Mexico, traveling for days with absolutely fine weather. Mr. Bangs and one other passenger chatted for hours about growing up in New England and about the possibility of war breaking out in Mexico. The brig itself hailed from Bangor, Maine. Meanwhile, Pillow, when he wasn't eating, continued to laze in the warm winter sun.

After rounding Key West, the *Carroll* entered the Gulf Stream, following its warm currents along the eastern coast of Florida and the coasts of Georgia and South Carolina. The passengers idled away the days by watching dolphins run alongside the ship and spotting flying fish as they leaped from the water. Mr. Bangs often sat on one of the hatch covers and wrote in his journal. The voyage had been uneventful. When he wasn't dozing on deck, Pillow lay on his master's bed below deck and slept.

The ship approached Cape Lookout, North Carolina, on the evening of February 8 after sailing for two weeks. As the *Carroll's* helmsman steered her northward, a dense fog enveloped her, making visibility poor. Although Captain Mitchell suspected he was close to Lookout Shoals, he had no idea just how close, for the heavy fog obscured the beam from the Cape Lookout Light. At 10:00 p.m., the *Carroll* struck one of the submerged shoals with a jarring impact, then lurched forward and finally ground to a halt, reeling over on her port side. Members of the crew on deck at the time tumbled head over heels, crashing into the ship's bulwarks. Mr. Bangs was thrown out of bed. And Pillow, awakened by the jolt, ran up on deck, only to also slide toward the bulwarks.

Then the *Carroll* began to slide over the bar and drifted into deep water. Several crew members quickly ran below to check for leakage. "She's still solid, Cap'n," one of them reported.

"Helmsman, steady as she goes," ordered Captain Mitchell.

"Captain, sir, the wheel isn't responding," replied the helmsman. "I don't think it's connected to the rudder." On closer investigation, the captain discovered that the *Carroll*'s rudder had indeed been ripped loose, leaving them with no way to control her.

Without a rudder, they had to rely on the wind, now blowing stronger from the southeast, to get the *Carroll* ashore before the sea overtook her. Surely, on this cold winter's night they would all perish if she foundered at sea. Not long after they gave the vessel over to the wind, the Cape Lookout light came into view about a mile distant.

"Shift the sails so we can see the light," ordered the captain. But hard as they tried, the crew just couldn't keep them in place with such a strong wind. Sailing almost blindly, the *Carroll* struck the shore a mile or so south of the lighthouse. Once grounded in shallow waters, it seemed that they might make it through the night if only they could survive the incessant beating by the sea.

At first light, the captain ordered, "Clear the lifeboat." As the crew lowered the boat a huge wave crashed into the side of the ship, capsizing the boat and smashing it in the breakers. By this time, the wind whipped up whitecaps on the swells. Even if they did manage to launch the boat, reaching shore at low tide while rowing against the wind in such a rough sea would be suicidal. Through all the commotion, Pillow hid in his

The dog paddled furiously, trying to stay above the water while the rope pulled tighter and tighter around his neck.

master's cabin while a cold rain began to pelt the deck.

Throughout the morning, Captain Mitchell and his crew tried to throw a line the forty yards to the beach, with no luck. A few local people appeared in late morning, but they could not figure a way to get a line out to the stranded vessel. By this time, the rain had turned to sleet that stung the faces of the passengers and crew and by noon it changed again to snow interspersed with hail. Wet and chilled to the bone, they huddled together for warmth as the force of the pounding breakers increased when the tide once again began to turn. The captain knew they had to do something soon.

"What about the dog?" asked a passenger. "Perhaps he could swim to shore with a line." The others agreed this might work, for none of them wanted to jump into the frigid water.

While one of the crewmen fetched the little dog, another tied a loop at the end of a piece of rope. Fastening it around Pillow's neck, the sailor carried him to the bow of the ship and, showing him the people on the beach, tossed him into the water. The dog paddled furiously, trying to stay above the water while the rope pulled tighter and tighter around his neck. At last he reached the snow-covered beach and ran into the waiting arms of one of the local men, who, with help from his neighbors, pulled the *Carroll*'s crew and passengers to safety. And though nearly frozen and suffering from exposure, all gave a hug of thanks to poor wet and shivering Pillow for saving their lives that cold, snowy January day.

4

Racer's Storm

Crowds of people milled around the wharf at the foot of Market Street in New York City amid piles of steamer trunks as some ninety passengers, many of them prominent and wealthy citizens, filed up the gangway onto the steam packet *Home* on the afternoon of October 7, 1837. Of those boarding, about thirty-five were women and children. The *Home* was due to sail with the tide at 4:00 p.m. for Charleston, South Carolina, with a crew of forty-five.

This was only the third trip to Charleston for the 550-ton side-wheeler steamboat. Built at a cost of $115,000 by Brown & Bell of New York for the Southern Steam Packet Company of New York, her hull had been launched on April 16, 1836, then towed to the Delancey Street iron works of James P. Allaire, who designed and installed the vessel's machinery. Sleek and trim, with only a twenty-two-foot beam, the *Home* could accommodate 120 passengers in berths or staterooms. The boat was originally built to ply eastern rivers, but Allaire converted her for coastal service before her maiden voyage. Though he finished the *Home* in January 1837, her first voyage didn't begin until April.

While she had a successful first trip, her second broke all records. She reached Charleston in sixty-four hours, and Allaire was confident his ship could beat her own record on her third voyage. There was so much excitement surrounding this trip that men placed bets on her. Several passengers came aboard just before departure, without even notifying their relatives, so that they could say they had sailed on the fastest steam packet afloat.

But the *Home's* third voyage wasn't to be the success everyone had hoped. The *Home* steamed out of New York Harbor guided by pilot E. C. Price aboard the steamboat *Isis*. Just past Governor's Island, he waved off the *Home* and her captain, Carleton White, took charge, placing a veteran helmsman at the wheel. But just an hour and a quarter out of port, a westerly wind and ebbing tide pushed the steam packet onto Romer Shoal, grounding her.

"Reverse engines," ordered Captain White. The *Home* stood her ground and, try as he might, just wouldn't budge. So the *Home* waited for high tide as her passengers enjoyed afternoon tea in the lounge. Then teatime stretched into supper, and it wasn't yet 10:30 p.m. when the high tide, assisted by steam and sail, lifted the ship off the shoal. Everyone knew that the *Home* had lost the opportunity to beat her own speed record.

By noon the following day, the wind velocity had increased substantially, producing large ocean swells. The sturdy steam packet chugged along, rolling gently over them.

At 7:30 p.m., Chief Engineer Hunt entered the wheelhouse. "Cap'n, one of the joints of the feeder pipe of the forward boiler has come apart."

"How bad is it?" asked Captain White.

"The leak is forcing more water into the hold than into the boiler," Hunt replied. "We need to pull in somewhere to repair her, sir."

"Helmsman, head for Chesapeake Bay," ordered the captain. Using only one boiler and a square sail, the *Home* limped into the shelter of the bay so that Hunt could repair the broken joint.

The engineer finished the job by midnight, and then the *Home* once again set sail under full steam south-southeast along the coast. But the farther the vessel traveled, the worse the weather became. By the time the *Home* reached Cape Hatteras, the wind had hit sixty-five miles per hour. At 9:00 a.m. on Monday, the engines stopped. Engineer Hunt once again entered the wheelhouse. "Cap'n, the feeder pipe has broken again, plus it looks like there's a leak in the floor under the boilers, perhaps damaged from when she ran aground." The ship began to wallow in the swells.

"Hoist the sails," ordered Captain White. "We've got to get her under control." As the sails filled, the helmsman was able to take control of the *Home* once again.

"If we can't get that pipe fixed, we'll have to run her aground on Wimble Shoals," said Captain White. But he never had to give that order, for as soon as Hunt repaired the broken pipe, the engines started and the *Home* headed out to sea.

Just as the ship turned east-southeast past Wimble Shoals, three giant breakers washed over her, breaking several windows, allowing water to pour into the cabins on her port side, and collapsing the aft gangway.

The weather continued to grow worse. Though Captain White knew he was in the midst of a storm at sea, he had no way of knowing that one of the worst hurricanes of the century, later known as Racer's Storm, was bearing down on the North Carolina coast. After originating south of Jamaica in September, it had produced a swath of devastation in the Yucatan and Texas's Gulf coast before turning east across Louisiana, Mississippi, Alabama, and Georgia, then curving north through South Carolina and up the coast.

By the morning of October 9, the *Home* ran into mammoth seas off Cape Hatteras and was taking on water faster than her pumps could handle it. Captain White gathered the passengers in the main cabin. "We need your help in bailing out the water," he said calmly. "Find whatever you can . . . buckets, pails, pans, kettles . . . and form a bucket brigade. We've got to lighten her." All pitched in, even the women, but the water poured in faster than they could bail it out.

Just after noon, Captain White thought he had safely passed Cape Hatteras. "Head due west," he ordered the helmsman. "We've got to beach her as soon as we can." The *Home* pitched to such a degree that her paddle wheels churned out of the water. No sooner had she climbed a wave than her bow fell violently into the ensuing trough.

At 2:00 p.m., Engineer Hunt reported to the captain, "The boat is leaking badly, sir. It won't be long until water reaches the fires."

"Send all available men to the pumps," ordered Captain White. "We must keep her afloat until we can beach her."

Water continued to flow into the aft hold. The crew

worked as hard as they could to keep the pumps going, but it seemed hopeless. Several inches of water sloshed across the engine-room floor, soaking the coal, so the firemen used wood to stoke the furnaces. The engine-room pumps became clogged with wet coal dust and stopped. Then the inevitable happened: The engines themselves stopped completely. Water had dampened the fires in the boilers.

"Raise the sails part way," ordered Captain White. "We'll guide her in under short sail."

Crewmen climbed the rigging as it whistled in the wind. But as soon as they had set the square sail, the wind tore it in half. Other sails flapped fiercely, some shredding as they tried to set them.

It was now 8:00 p.m. as the *Home* passed around Diamond Shoals, within several miles of the beach.

The hurricane winds whipped up furious seas that tossed the vessel violently. Giant waves rose high above her upper deck. Passengers and crew could barely stand as she rolled and pitched in the strong winds. The amount of water in the *Home's* hold caused her to move slowly. Observing the heavy breakers, Captain White knew it would be difficult to beach her.

"Turn her to port," White ordered the helmsman, "and make sure to stand clear of the wheel when she strikes, lest it break your bones."

The *Home* ran aground on the outer reef one hundred yards from the dimly lit beach northeast of Ocracoke Village at 10:00 p.m. The force of the strike turned her northward, exposing her deck and upper houses to the gigantic waves. The sudden jolt on impact sent crew and passengers alike into a panic. Those huddled on the landward side of the ship were instantly washed overboard.

"Women and children to the forecastle," the captain shouted. Here, the upper deck would offer them protection from the incessant breakers that lashed the grounded vessel.

"Man the lifeboats," ordered Captain White. The *Home* carried only three lifeboats and two life preservers for 130 people. One had been destroyed at sea, and as several crewmen tried to launch another, the roiling sea broke it into pieces in midair. They did manage to lower the third, filled with about twenty frightened people. Unfortunately, it got only a short distance away before it overturned, dumping its occupants into the tumultuous surf.

Two seamen grabbed the life preservers, and though washed overboard by a huge wave, they managed to get to shore. Through all this pandemonium, the soulful sound of the ship's bell, rung by passenger Andrew A. Lovegreen, called out for help.

Less than an hour after striking and under constant pounding from the sea, the *Home* broke into three pieces. The forecastle broke loose and drifted into the surf, tossing the women and children gathered there into the raging sea, which muffled their screams of terror as they disappeared beneath the waves. Lovegreen also dropped into the water and struggled to shore.

The hurricane continued to ravage the ship. Tremendous waves tore apart her timbers and planks. With a loud crack, the mainmast snapped, raining her rigging, spars, and torn sails down on her deck. With a fierce boom that made the entire vessel shudder, a giant breaker knocked over one of her smokestacks, crushing a mother cradling her infant son in her arms. Another crashed into the dining cabin, and a third destroyed the starboard staterooms. Then the upper deck separated from the hull. Through it all, the *Home's* bell continued to toll. By the time it was all over, only the ship's boiler stood above the water.

Mighty hurricane-driven combers, containing pieces of the wreck, some with dazed survivors lashed to them, churned up onto the beach for miles. Lifeless bodies of those less fortunate tumbled onto the sands in grotesque poses. Captain White, who himself had drifted to shore on a piece of wreckage, crawled up onto the sand. Five or six others did likewise.

After gaining their composure, several headed toward Ocracoke Light, about seven miles down the beach, while the remaining searched for survivors along the beach. The searchers, led by Captain White, hadn't traveled far when they met Andrew Lovegreen, who had survived his swim through the tumultuous surf. Lovegreen hugged Captain White, happy that they had survived.

By Captain White's final tally only forty persons—himself, twenty passengers including a twelve-year-old boy, and nineteen crewmen—had survived. In amongst the piles of soaked clothing lay the body of an infant. Ninety-five others, including James B. Allaire, the owner's nephew, lost their lives. While they waited for help on the sand, some ate pears and apples that had washed up from the wreck.

As dawn broke over the scene, the survivors gazed at dead bodies dressed in fine silks, some bedecked in jewels, lying

The hurricane continued to ravage the ship . . .

among the littered remains of the *Home*. Not long after, a rescue party from the village arrived with blankets and food. They took the survivors—who were eventually transported to Wilmington, North Carolina, by boat—back to town to stay with residents. Captain White stayed in Ocracoke for a month and a half, overseeing the burial of the bodies and the gathering of passenger belongings that could be salvaged from the debris.

The wreck of the *Home* forced steam packet companies to equip their vessels with more life preservers. And in 1838, Congress passed the Steamboat Act, which made it mandatory for all ships to have enough life preservers for all onboard.

5

Shipboard Romance

Charles Ridge, a young man in his early twenties from New Orleans, had been looking forward to his voyage aboard the *Pulaski*, a luxurious packet steamer on its regular run from Savannah, Georgia, to Baltimore, Maryland, by way of Charleston, South Carolina. Rather shy, he had remained by himself since the vessel set sail from Savannah on the morning of June 13, 1838, with ninety passengers and thirty-seven crewmen.

Later that afternoon, the *Pulaski* docked at Charleston. The early summer air felt warm as sixty-five more passengers boarded. Among them was Catherine Onslow, also in her early twenties. Her presence hadn't gone unnoticed: As Mr. Ridge stood by the railing watching the passengers come aboard, he caught her eye and knew that he had to meet her.

After taking on additional passengers, the *Pulaski* immediately got underway. An air of congeniality seemed to envelop the ship as passengers introduced themselves to each other while they strolled about the deck and took in the warm evening air under a velvety sky filled with twinkling stars.

Meanwhile, First Mate Hibbert had gone below to take a short nap before his nightly watch. Captain Dubois had guided the *Pulaski* along the shore until she reached Cape Romain. After that, he then turned the ship over to his second captain, Ronald Pearson, who directed her out to sea.

Built by John A. Robb of Baltimore for the Savannah & Charleston Steam Packet Company of Savannah, the 680-ton side-wheeler *Pulaski* had been plying her route between Savannah/Charleston and Norfolk/Baltimore less than eight months. With a potential of nearly two hundred horsepower, she was both fast and luxurious, with three cabins housing berths for 116 passengers and four staterooms for families. She also had a reputation for fine food, expertly served.

Mr. Ridge could feel the throbbing of the *Pulaski*'s engine as she entered the open ocean. As he gazed out over the water from his deck chair, he began to feel the ship pitching and rolling as the sea swells increased in height from the easterly wind. Each time the *Pulaski* plowed into one, great fans of spray washed over her bow.

Down below, the boiler room crew stoked the coal fires to keep the engine running at full steam. As dusk fell upon the ship, the wind let up a bit, but the vessel continued to pitch and roll, causing many of the passengers to hurriedly dash for the rail. Seasickness prevented them from enjoying their evening meal, so most sought the comfort of their berths.

First Mate Hibbert took over the night watch at 10:30 p.m. from Mr. Pearson. Captain Dubois lay sleeping on a mattress in the corner. With the shipboard lights dimmed, the stars shone brightly in the black sky. Most of the passengers had long since fallen asleep to the rocking motion of the ship. Most except Mr. Ridge, who sat in his deck chair fantasizing about the young woman he had seen boarding that afternoon.

Major James Heath, a passenger from Charleston on his way to his berth, thought the pressure showing on the gauge of one of the boilers to be abnormally high, but the second engineer, Mr. Chicken, assured him it was well within safe limits. So Major Heath continued on through the aft cabin to his berth, being careful not to wake anyone as he readied himself for a good night's sleep.

Not thirty minutes later, Mr. Chicken turned the water-cock on that boiler. A shrill whistle, indicating that the water in the boiler was too low, pierced the ship, alerting First Mate Hibbert in the wheelhouse. *I've got to warn the second engineer not to add water until the temperature in the boiler goes down,* he thought. But as he raced to warn the engineer, a loud explosion rocked the ship, hurtling Hibbert onto the main deck, knocking him unconscious.

The boiler had exploded, shattering the starboard side of the *Pulaski* amidships. At the same time, it blew off the promenade deck above and collapsed the forward cabin, blocking the stairway to it.

Jolted awake by the sound of the explosion, Major Heath tried to run back through the aft cabin, but a spray of scalding steam prevented him from doing so. He took shelter under the steps until the steam subsided. As he made his way through the cabin, he saw some passengers killed instantly as they slept while others lay frozen in horror as the hot steam killed them in their attempt to escape.

In the meantime, Mr. Hibbert regained consciousness; though dazed, he wasn't injured. Stumbling aft, he discovered a hole in the ship's starboard side where the sea now poured in when the *Pulaski* rolled that way. The heaviness of the port boiler helped keep the ship afloat—for the time being.

By this time, the remaining passengers were running screaming onto the deck. During the explosion, Captain Dubois must have been hurled into the sea and drowned, for he was nowhere to be found. The absence of Mr. Pearson, who was off duty and had gone below to sleep, left only First Mate Hibbert in charge. "Lower the lifeboats," he ordered. *I'll tell the passengers that we're going to inspect the damage,* he thought, *that way they won't panic and storm the lifeboats.* Calmly, Hibbert undid the lines holding the starboard yawl, and, with help from Mr. Ridge, lowered it into the sea. Then he climbed aboard and motioned for two of the male passengers to come with him to man the oars. Slowly they backed away from the ship, plucking passengers and crewmen from the rolling sea.

Crewman Elias N. Barney, assisted by several passengers, had, by this time, lowered the port yawl into the water. Several others threw one of the smaller boats overboard, but its wood had dry-rotted, causing it to flood immediately and sink. Both Barney and Hibbert continued to rescue people from the water until both of their boats were full. "Let's head for shore, sir," Barney said to Hibbert. The occupants of the third boat—two crewmen and ten passengers—had to bail furiously to keep it afloat as it was in almost as bad condition as the one that had already sunk.

"No, Mr. Barney," replied Hibbert. "We shall stay by the ship and rescue as many people as we can."

While Mr. Ridge was helping First Mate Hibbert with the boat, he spied the young woman who had first drawn his attention and went to help her into the boat. But in the confusion, he lost her in the crowd of panicking passengers. As he desperately searched for her, the mast snapped with a sharp crack and toppled over into the water, crushing one of the passengers. Minutes later the *Pulaski* broke in two with a loud splintering sound, and Mr. Ridge was tossed overboard. The part of the deck forward of the mast drifted away and began to sink.

Mr. Ridge scrambled back onto the deck. He quickly took two of the settees from the aft cabin and a large cask and lashed them together with pieces of torn sail to form a raft for himself. The ship was just beginning to sink beneath the waves. It was 11:45 p.m. and nearly half of the people on board had drowned, been crushed by falling masts, or been scalded to death.

As Mr. Ridge settled on the raft, he saw a woman thrashing around in the water not far away. He jumped in and swam to her rescue, returning her to his raft. It wasn't until they got themselves onto the raft, with only their heads and shoulders above the water, that he realized it was the same young woman he had been watching since she first arrived on board.

"Thank you for saving me," she said. "I'm Miss Onslow . . . Catherine Onslow. But this raft isn't big enough for the two of us. You'll have to let me go to save yourself."

"Nonsense," said Mr. Ridge. "I'll hear none of that. We either live or die together."

"Nonsense," said Mr. Ridge. "I'll hear none of that. We either live or die together."

After floating around in the darkness for a while, they discovered a section of the ship's decking and with much effort pulled the settees on top of it. Soon Mr. Barney's boat drifted by but it was already full.

"Please take Miss Onslow with you," pleaded Mr. Ridge.

"No, I cannot leave you here alone," replied Miss Onslow. So they continued to drift on by themselves.

As the sun crept above the horizon the next morning, Mr. Ridge thought he saw land not far away, but their raft seemed to be drifting in the opposite direction, toward the open sea. Not long after, the land disappeared and they drifted aimlessly for another night and day. As they drifted along, exhausted and starving, they pledged their love for each other in life and in death.

Miss Onslow thought she saw a ship coming toward them as morning dawned on the third day. They frantically waved their arms and soon realized that they were going to be rescued. Though terribly sunburned and dehydrated, they were able to climb aboard the rescue ship.

As they stepped from the ship onto the dock, Mr. Ridge confessed to his newfound love. "I've lost everything," he said. "I'm penniless. So I release you from our vow."

The young woman, tears streaming down her cheeks, said, "Poverty can never drive us to a more desperate extreme than that which we have suffered together in the last few days. I love you now and I always will."

With that, the couple's engagement became official, and they got married soon afterward. After they both said "I do" and kissed, Miss Onslow made a confession of her own. "Charles, I meant to tell you that I'm the heiress to a $200,000 fortune."

6

Of Human Flesh

ORLINE ST. JOHN—1854

It was February 16, 1854. A black seaman named Douglass hoisted his seaman's chest up on his shoulder and stepped aboard the 250-ton barkentine *Orline St. John* docked in Norfolk Harbor. In the next few hours he and his fellow crewmen would be preparing the ship for her long voyage to Barbados. Captain Redbird escorted his new wife aboard, her parasol protecting her from the rays of the sun, and got her settled in his cabin. As with many captains' wives, she had decided to sail with her new husband aboard his cargo ship.

William Bradstreet of Gardiner, Massachusetts, owner of the *Orline St. John,* had her built in 1848. She had served as a cargo ship, traveling from northern ports to southern ones and beyond.

For the first few days, the ship sailed over somewhat ordinary seas. But on the morning of February 20 the wind began to blow hard. By midday a howling gale blew against the ship's starboard beam. The strong wind filled out the *Orline*'s sails as she tacked to starboard. The following day she would be off Cape Hatteras. Suddenly, the wind became blustery, causing the vessel to groan under the strain and lay over on her starboard beam ends. Then, as the wind shifted, she turned the other way until she was almost lying on her port beam ends. As the bark righted herself the second time, the full force of that gale caught her sails against their forward side. The main brace supporting the large mainmast snapped under the strain, and the huge mast came toppling down on the deck, bringing a confused mass of sails and rigging with it.

The fierce winds had doomed the *Orline St. John*. She lay dead in the water with her huge mast trailing overside. Her helm was unresponsive. The only hope now was to drop both anchors and pray that they would hold the ship off the leeward shore. "Drop the anchors," ordered Captain Redbird. The anchors bit into the ocean bottom and brought the stricken vessel's head up into the gale wind. For a short time the anchors held.

But the force of the wind and sea was too much for the bark, and together they dragged the ship until the anchors broke loose, letting her wallow in the heavy seas. That night the situation worsened as the seas became heavier, sweeping over the foundering vessel, almost completely filling the cabin and drowning a black seaman named Martin. Every wave breaking over the *Orline*'s starboard side swept all the way over her decks, from starboard to port. The temperature of the sea water had fallen below freezing, and each breaker added to the sheet of ice steadily forming on the portions of the ship still above the water.

That night the wind shifted abruptly to the northwest and increased in velocity. The temperature dipped even lower.

Meanwhile, the captain's wife, Hannah, became trapped in the cabin. "Help me free her," shouted the captain. Together he and several crewmen managed to pull the frightened woman through a small window. They carried her out onto the deck and hauled her up into part of the rigging still standing. "Lash her to the spar," he cried, "then lash yourselves to whatever you can." By this time, the storm-driven seas regularly swept over the deck of the vessel.

"Take what refuge you can in the rigging that's left," the captain ordered his crew. "Lash yourselves tight." Obedient and well-disciplined to the end, they obeyed his order without hesitation. Up the slippery foremast all seven of them climbed, in an effort to get above the reach of the icy waves. They lashed themselves with rope as securely as their numbed fingers would allow and waited for their fate. The sea below them had now become a boiling cauldron of angry waves lashed by the ever-changing wind.

By the following afternoon, February 22, Hannah died in her husband's arms. He and several crewmen lowered her body into the sea, which immediately swallowed her. That same night the second mate, who had been drinking salt water, became delirious. As he tried to enter the cabin to get some fresh water, the captain shouted, "Lash yourself, man, before you get swept away." And just as the words came out of the captain's mouth, a huge wave engulfed the deck and the seaman disappeared.

The cold and wet were more than some could bear, and the following day seaman Douglass died in the rigging from exposure. Helpless to save him and intent on saving themselves, the

They lashed themselves with rope as securely as their numbed fingers would allow and waited for their fate.

captain and the remainder of his crew left his body to hang there.

For a full week the captain, first mate, and several seamen, without access to food or water and suffering from cold and exposure, remained in the rigging of the drifting ship. At last their instinct for survival overpowered them, and they began to feed on Douglass's body.

As the days wore on, the now nearly frozen men saw several vessels pass nearby, but the fierce gale and heavy seas immediately drove them off. On March 1, eight days after the *Orline St. John* lost its mainmast, another bark, the *Saxonville*, on its way from Calcutta to Boston, appeared on the horizon. Seeing the state of the wrecked ship through his looking glass, the captain of the *Saxonville* ordered his helmsman to set a course straight for her. With dogged persistence, the captain and crew rescued the forlorn sailors.

Upon arrival in Boston Harbor, the *Saxonville*'s captain immediately summoned a doctor. He amputated both feet of Thomas Grant, one of the survivors of the wrecked ship, who had suffered from severe frostbite and gangrene from his feet being continually in salt water. While all the others suffered from similar maladies, none seemed to experience any ill effects from eating the flesh of their dead shipmate, Douglass.

7

The Plight of the Drunken Captain

POCAHONTAS—1862

It had been nine months since the Confederates fired on Fort Sumter in Charleston, South Carolina. Since then, Colonel Ambrose Burnside had developed a bold plan of attack against territory held by the Confederates. The plan, which attracted the attention of President Abraham Lincoln, was to fit out chartered steamboats, barges, and other sailing vessels with nearly fifteen thousand soldiers from regiments from northeastern coastal states. One of the steam packet boats involved was the side-wheeler *Pocahontas*.

After her launching in 1829, the *Pocahontas*, built by Beacham & Gardiner of Baltimore, Maryland, ferried passengers from Baltimore to Norfolk and Richmond in under seventeen hours. She was strictly first class all the way, allowing her passengers to travel in elegant comfort in finely furnished cabins, with men below deck and women in special cabins on the main deck. Her dining room could hold up to one hundred people. The boilers for her one-hundred-horsepower engine sat below, a new innovation at the time. Her owners boasted that she could travel at twelve miles per hour without a feeling of motion. Should her passengers wish to take a stroll on nicer days to catch views of Chesapeake Bay, the *Pocahontas* offered an upper deck that ran the width and length of the ship.

The *Pocahontas* alternately traveled between Baltimore and Richmond with her sister ship, the *Columbus*. With the age of steam came scheduled departures and arrivals, something that traditional sailing ships just couldn't offer. Passengers paid $7 for the trip, including meals, and could travel between Norfolk and Richmond for just $3.

Throughout her illustrious career, *Pocahontas* had several owners. By 1840, some of the steamship lines had merged because of the increasing competition from the railroads. The Baltimore Steam Packet Company, which took ownership of the *Pocahontas*, overhauled her, mounting two boilers on deck and adding a vertical beam engine. The Powhatan Steam Boat Company, a subsidiary of the larger Baltimore Steam Packet Company, took her over in 1841 to carry passengers between Norfolk and Richmond. By 1848, the ship needed repair, so the company rebuilt her, increasing her tonnage by 184 tons. The *Pocahontas* continued on her runs between Norfolk and Richmond until the onset of the Civil War.

On July 25, 1861, the U.S. Quarter Master Department chartered the *Pocahontas* for $225 per day. Eventually, it raised the rate to $450. On January 7, 1862, the department attached the boat to the fleet of steamboats assembled by Burnside, now a general, paying her owners $550 per day. Burnside's diverse group of boats and barges became known as the Burnside Expedition. He ordered water-tight compartments added to them, as well as heavy oak planking, and had sandbags piled in low walls around four to six large guns on their decks.

On the morning of January 9, 1862, the Burnside Expedition set sail with over eighty converted boats. The once-elegant steamboat's dining room and decks became a traveling stable for 103 horses belonging to the Fourth Rhode Island Infantry and the Twenty-fifth Massachusetts Infantry. Also riding on board were sixty wagon drivers, grooms, and mechanics.

Burnside kept the ultimate destination of his expedition secret even from the ships' captains since, with spies infiltrating both sides, no one could be trusted. Many of the captains assumed that Norfolk, now under Confederate control, was the objective of the expedition. The boats gathered at the mouth of the Chesapeake to await further orders.

On the evening of January 11, Burnside ordered his fleet into the Atlantic, with specific instructions for the captains not to open their sealed orders until after they passed Cape Henry. It was then that they learned that Burnside intended to invade Roanoke Island on the Outer Banks in North Carolina. To reach the island, they knew they had to go around dangerous Diamond Shoals and enter Pamlico Sound through Hatteras Inlet.

Aware of the dangers that lay ahead of them, several of the ships' captains refused to sail into the Atlantic Ocean, claiming that their vessels were unseaworthy. In truth, none of the captains had experience operating their steamers on the open sea. The captain of the *Pocahontas* was used to running his steamboat routinely along the placid waters of the James River. He had been rumored to have a drinking problem as well. And the steamboat's pilot only had experience guiding her through shallow waters. Neither man was prepared for what lay ahead.

Those ships that did venture ahead towed converted barges and canal boats. Once they reached the open ocean, they struggled to keep the overloaded barges under control. As the swells became higher and the troughs lower, the barges began to take on water. One of them, the *Grapeshot,* parted her tow line, separating her from her towing ship. Her crew jumped overboard as men on her towing ship, the *New Brunswick,* quickly threw ropes out to them and pulled them to safety. The *Grapeshot* headed straight for shore, where it ran aground north of Cape Hatteras, dumping its load of hay and oats.

Unfortunately, the *Pocahontas* didn't depart with the rest of the expedition. She had been detained at Fortress Monroe until January 16 for repairs. She had sailed for over thirty years and hadn't been overhauled in fourteen. By the time she made it to the mouth of the Chesapeake, a storm with gale force winds had moved into the area. Unbeknownst to her captain, two of the fleet's ships had already sunk and the barge *Grapeshot* had run aground.

By the following evening, when one of her rudder chains broke, the *Pocahontas* had sailed twenty-five miles from Cape Henry. "Stop the engine," ordered her captain. "Drop anchor in this trough so we can repair the damages." To some of his crew the captain seemed a bit tipsy, but there was so much going on at the time that no one gave it a second thought.

But as the ship approached Cape Hatteras, his orders got more bizarre. He would give one command then immediately

The Pocahontas's *pilot sailed her toward shore until she struck a shoal.*

reverse it. Suddenly a previous patch on the boiler blew, sending hot steam rushing throughout the ship with a loud hiss. "Stop the engine!" he shouted. This time it was so the ship's carpenter could drive a pine plug into the hole. Meanwhile, the captain retired to his cabin for another drink. As soon as everything was under control, the *Pocahontas* got under way, but the captain didn't appear on the bridge. They hadn't traveled but three miles when the other rudder chain broke, thus compromising the pilot's ability to steer the *Pocahontas*. With only one rudder, the pilot couldn't fully control where the ship went. Soon after, a loud crash echoed throughout the boat as the grating in the boiler room fell, dousing the fire in the boiler. This was followed by another crash as the smoke-pipe blew down.

"Set sail and head for the beach," ordered the ship's pilot. The captain lay in a drunken stupor on the floor of his cabin. At this point, neither the captain nor the pilot could do much to save her.

Sure that the boat was going to sink, but not knowing that they were still ten miles from shore, the grooms led the horses on deck to the gangway and pushed them overboard in hopes that they would swim to safety. Those tied up below deck weren't so lucky. So intent were the teamsters on saving themselves that they refused to go below and cut the horses loose.

Meanwhile, the *Pocahontas*'s pilot sailed her toward shore until she struck a shoal. After that, the breakers promptly began chopping her to pieces. The men on board reached shore safely on their own. Since the outbreak of the Civil War the lifesaving service had been suspended, so the men of the

Pocahontas had to rely on the help of local residents. The nineteen horses that made it to shore found hay and oats, spilled by the *Grapeshot,* on the beach.

And there on January 18, 1862, on a shoal off Kinnakeet, the once-elegant *Pocahontas* met her demise, all because her captain was too drunk to take charge.

8

The Lifesaver's Widow

NUOVA OTTAVIA—1876

The first day of March 1876 began like every other day for Molly Berry Gray and her two children. Her son, Spencer Jr., had just returned from fetching a bucket of water so she could brew some tea. Her little daughter sat and played with her dolly in front of the fireplace. Six months pregnant, Molly had begun to feel the weight of her unborn child in her back. She and her husband, Spencer, had lived on Church's Island across Pamlico Sound from the Currituck Light ever since they had married. Spencer had worked as a fisherman, carpenter, hunter, and farmer—just about anything to support his growing family. But when Molly found out she was pregnant with their third child, he had to find steady work that paid more. The only job that paid high wages was as a surfman in the new United States Lifesaving Service.

Molly begged her husband not to join the crew at the Currituck Light, but she realized he had no other choice if they were to raise a third child. So Spencer had crossed the sound and moved into the Jones Hill Lifesaving Station the previous October.

Balding and hunched with a slight middle-age slump, Spencer had become used to walking the lonely patrols along the beach north and south of the station in all kinds of weather. When he wasn't on patrol, he and his fellow surfmen sat and waited. The Service paid him a handsome twenty dollars a month—the highest pay for any job on the Outer Banks at the time—to save the lives of seamen and passengers trapped on wrecks out on the shoals. He had learned how to fire the Lyle gun, set up the breeches buoy and life car, and how to help launch and row the station's lifeboat in rough seas. But he couldn't get used to being away from Molly and his two children. It seemed he missed them more every day, even though he did get to visit with them from time to time.

Though the wind blew lightly from the southeast on the evening of March 1, the sea rolled in big combers that pounded the beach hard. As darkness fell, Keeper John G. Gale of the Jones Hills station spotted what he believed to be a large ship, perhaps a bark, off in the haze. He thought he heard the flapping of her sails, but just faintly over the roar of the surf. He couldn't tell exactly how far the vessel, which might be stranded, was from the shore, but he guessed it had to be at least two hundred yards. The combination of dim light at the end of the day and the haze prevented him from knowing if her decks were awash or above water or if she had begun to break apart. And he couldn't tell if anyone remained onboard.

Both the Jones Hills station and its keeper were relatively new to the Service. In fact, the U.S. Lifesaving Service was having growing pains and hadn't yet enforced strict training and experience requirements for its keepers and crews. Because of the onset of darkness and the nighttime fog, Keeper Gale couldn't be confident in using the Lyle gun to fire a line to the vessel. To be sure, he'd have to wait until daylight, and then it might be too late. Rowing out in the surfboat seemed the only solution.

"Haul out the lifeboat," ordered Gale without hesitation. Only five of his crew responded—Malachi Brumsey, Lemuel Griggs, Jerry Munden, Lewis White, and Spencer Gray. He had sent a sixth, John Chappell, to Tulls Creek that afternoon for supplies, and he hadn't yet returned. The men pulled the heavy boat down to the breakers, pushed it in, jumped in, and manned the oars.

By this time, the commotion made by the surfmen had attracted several onlookers, including H. T. Halstead, J. W. Lewis, and George W. Wilson, each offering to help. "I'm short a man," said Keeper Gale. "Would one of you men like to go out in the boat with us?" Halstead, an older and smaller man, volunteered and gingerly climbed into the surfboat. "Hold on there," said Gale. "I think we need a younger, larger man." George Wilson stepped forward, exchanging places with Halstead, then the crew rowed out through the haze over the rolling sea to the ship.

The six surfmen and Wilson had their work cut out for them. Spencer Gray kept his head low as he used all his strength to pull on his oar. But Gale had forgotten to remind them to wear their cork life vests, which hung on pegs back at the station. As they drew closer to the vessel, Gale could tell it was indeed a fully rigged bark, its sails flapping loudly in the breeze. There, written across her stern, was the name *Nuova*

The men pulled the heavy boat down to the breakers, pushed it in, jumped in, and manned the oars.

Ottavia. She had run aground on a nearby shoal.

Anxiously, the group of onlookers, which had by now grown in size with the addition of their neighbors in Currituck, watched the lifeboat bob through the surf to the calmer sea beyond and finally disappear into the night. Now all they could see was the faint glow of the lantern at the back of the boat as it rose and fell with the heavy ocean swells. All they could hear was the roar of the breakers as they crashed upon the beach and the muffled flapping of the *Ottavia*'s sails.

Meanwhile, as Keeper Gale carefully steered the lifeboat closer to the ship, he and his crew heard cries for help from the Italian sailors. The surfmen lifted their oars and drifted in next to the stricken vessel. Before any of them had time to do anything, the frightened Italian crew jumped into the boat. Gale felt the surfboat begin to roll but couldn't stop it. In a matter of seconds, the rolling movement capsized the boat, dumping all on board into the sea. Keeper Gale, three surfmen, and five Italian sailors became trapped under it and drowned. Jerry Munden and Spencer Gray and five of the sailors managed to climb back aboard the *Nuova Ottavia*.

The people on the beach heard a terrified scream off in the darkness. Then the lantern light vanished. The roar of the surf continued unabated. They stared into the night but saw nothing. All of a sudden one of the lifeboat oars washed ashore, followed by another, then another, and another. A little while later, the lifeboat itself drifted in upside down. They waited and stared into the darkness, helplessly, for several hours. Finally, the lifeless body of surfman Malachi Brumsey, his skin blue and his body bloated, washed up on the beach.

By the time daylight arose, members of some of the surf-men's families had joined the others on the beach. The *Nuova Ottavia* appeared as the haze lifted, its masts still standing. Eight men stood huddled together on her deck, among them Spencer Gray. They recognized his bald head and unmistakable slump. They were sure of one thing: Keeper Gale wasn't among them. Sometime later, his body washed up, along with those of Lewis White, Lemuel Griggs, and volunteer George Wilson, plus five unidentified seamen, obviously members of the *Ottavia*'s crew.

Try as they might, the people on shore couldn't do much but wait for the inevitable to happen. Even though the ship lay within range of the Lyle gun and though they had a more than ample supply of shot and line, none of the bystanders knew how to use them to rescue the stranded men. They tried several times anyway but the gun became clogged with sand. When that didn't work, they sent rocket after rocket into the sky throughout the day—forty-one in all—to let those remaining on the vessel, especially Spencer Gray, know that they were trying to help them.

But by noon the *Nuova Ottavia* began to break up. By 2:00 p.m., she had vanished beneath the surface. An hour or so later, four members of her crew drifted ashore clinging to a piece of wreckage. Those waiting on the shore rushed to help them, pulling the bruised and exhausted survivors from the surf. Two had open wounds on their feet received from rubbing against spikes exposed from the breaking deck. None of them spoke English, making it hard for the residents to find out exactly what happened to the bark. The bodies of surfmen

Jerry Munden and Spencer Gray never washed ashore.

The lifesavers from Jones Hill station became the first to die in service. The $408 in gold awarded to their families in recognition of their heroism by the Italian Department of Foreign Affairs and Marine at the request of the Italian Society for Salvage did little to comfort those left behind, especially Molly Gray, now a widow with two children to support and a third on the way.

9

Bad Luck Friday

HURON—1877

Superstitious sailors won't put to sea on Friday. They say it brings bad luck. Lieutenant Arthur H. Fletcher was one of those sailors. As Executive Officer of the converted gunship *Huron*, due to sail out of Hampton Roads, Virginia, shortly after noon on Friday, November 23, he had refused to report for duty, saying that he had had a premonition of disaster. After repeated requests for a transfer, he had deserted and had been thrown into the brig. Taking Fletcher's place onboard was Lieutenant S. A. Simmons, for whom superstitions meant nothing.

Ensign Lucian Young, a twenty-five-year-old navy man from Lexington, Kentucky, also believed in no such superstition and prepared to sail on the *Huron*. His sea chest contained a medal awarded him by the Humane Society of the City of New York and a letter of commendation from the Secretary of the Navy for distinguished bravery in jumping overboard to rescue a seaman who had fallen out of the rigging during a severe storm. But this short, stout sailor didn't look like a hero.

On this particular Friday the barkentine-rigged screw-steamer *Huron* was the only vessel in Hampton Roads cleared for sea duty. Storm warnings had been flying at Norfolk and Cape Henry since Wednesday afternoon. Captains of all the other vessels in port had battened down the hatches to ride out the impending storm.

Looking out at the threatening gray sky, Commander George P. Ryan, captain of the *Huron,* pondered his orders, which told him to set sail as soon as draftsman John J. Evans, who was to assist in a survey of the Cuban coast, arrived from Washington, D.C. Ryan, a veteran navigator and seaman, had personally chosen his officers from some of the best in the Navy. He ran a tight ship, demanding that every man follow his orders to the letter.

Workmen laid the keel of the *Huron,* named after one of the Great Lakes, at the Delaware River Shipbuilding Company in Chester, Pennsylvania, in 1873. Her hull, built of ⅝-inch iron, had been dubbed "the strongest in the Atlantic." She received her commission on November 15, 1875. Designated a third-rate gunboat, meaning she carried a third less armament than a first-rate ship, the 541-ton *Huron* had iron plating and schooner-rigged sails. Her ordinance included five large smoothbore guns, a Gatling gun, and an assortment of small arms. She also carried a number of small boats: two launches, a cutter, a whaleboat, a dinghy, a gig, and two life rafts called balsas. Her simple two-cylinder steam engine, powered by five boilers, could drive the ship at ten knots.

Shipyard workers at the New York Navy Yard refitted the *Huron* from August to October 1877. In early November,

Ryan sailed her to Hampton Roads, where she lay at anchor for three days while being loaded with coal for her long voyage. Commander Ryan hadn't received his orders concerning Evans until the night before the *Huron*'s regularly scheduled departure. The following morning she passed inspection and made ready for sea with 115 crewmen and sixteen officers aboard while Ryan waited for Evans.

As soon as Evans arrived, Ryan headed his ship south past the mouth of the Chesapeake Bay. The wind blew harder, churning up the sea. The *Huron* passed several ships heading for the shelter of Hampton Roads as it continued to steam toward the open ocean. "Set the sails against a forty-knot wind," Ryan ordered, "and reduce speed to five knots."

At 6:30 p.m., the *Huron* passed Currituck Beach, with Currituck Light eight miles off the starboard beam. The fog grew so thick that only the sounding lead kept Commander Ryan apprised of his position.

"Maintain a steady course, south-southeast," Ryan ordered his helmsman. "Keep her close to shore." In setting his course southward, Commander Ryan chose to sail close to the North Carolina shoreline to avoid traveling against the Gulf Stream or taking the time-consuming and longer alternative of going out beyond it. As in so many cases off the Carolina coast, his decision proved fatal.

Suddenly, a storm with gale-force winds struck and carried away the *Huron*'s staysail. "Secure the sails," ordered Lieutenant W. P. Conway, on watch at that time, "and take soundings." He learned from the leadsman that the *Huron* was in fifteen fathoms of water.

Lieutenant James M. Wright relieved Conway at 8:00 p.m. and reported nothing out of the ordinary when he handed the duty over to Lieutenant W. S. French at midnight. Currituck Light had since faded into the fog, and the beam from the Bodie Island Light had yet to pierce the thick mist. Both Wright and French believed the ship to be a safe distance from shore. Since the North Carolina coast bends slightly to the east just before Kitty Hawk, a small course change is necessary. But they made no such change.

Shortly after 1:00 a.m., without warning of any kind, the *Huron* suddenly came to a grinding halt, catapulting sleeping crewmen from their hammocks. At first it appeared that the ship had run aground on an uncharted shoal eight miles or so offshore, but then the lookout sang out, "Breakers to starboard." French faintly spotted land through the dark, swirling mist.

"Hard over," Lieutenant French shouted to the helmsman. "Leadsman take soundings." But his orders came too late; the *Huron* swung around toward the beach, heeling over on her port side. The ship had come ashore on Bodie Island without her officers ever seeing Bodie Island Light.

Lieutenant Conway, awakened by the shock of the ship striking, thought she had collided with some other vessel. Commander Ryan rushed on deck, charts in hand. "What's our location, Mr. French?" he asked.

"I don't know, sir," French replied.

"Give the order for all hands on deck."

"Aye, sir."

By 1:30 a.m., Ensign Young had taken his place near the

Captain, awaiting further orders. Though officers and crew members ran to their stations, there was neither confusion nor hysteria. Ryan's choice of officers and his sense of discipline had paid off. When the mist parted, Commander Ryan finally saw the North Carolina coastline. "My God! How did we get in here?" he cried.

For the next several hours, huge waves continued to bombard the *Huron's* five-eights-inch-thick hull, washing over her exposed deck. The seas broke over the vessel from her port side. First the foremast, then the main topmast broke away, creating a tangled mass of rigging and broken spars on the deck. Water poured down the open hatches. "Batten down the hatches, throw the guns overboard, and take in the sails!" ordered Commander Ryan. But his orders were in vain since the few hatch covers that remained had broken, the guns were too firmly attached to the deck to be dislodged, and those men who had climbed aloft couldn't make headway with the sails because of the strong winds. The steam whistle bleated hoarsely, but the cacophony of raging wind and churning sea absorbed the feeble blasts so that no one would hear it to respond.

"Launch the boats!" shouted Lieutenant French. Lieutenant Conway assembled a crew and directed efforts to get the cutter overboard. But before it could be cleared of the ship's side, the forward davit bored a hole into it, and as it struck the water a huge wave carried it away. Though the cutter rode back on the next swell, it smashed into a stanchion, which tore another hole in its side. Conway and his helpers, though helpless to secure the smaller boat, did manage to

Without warning of any kind, the Huron suddenly came to a grinding halt, catapulting sleeping crewmen from their hammocks.

attach a line to its bow so that if it did reach shore, the line might serve as a means of rescuing those left behind. But this was a futile exercise, as water poured in through the holes in the cutter's side, and it filled and sank.

By this time the tide had receded, so the *Huron*'s officers believed they had a good chance of freeing the stranded gunboat by backing her engines. Though the firemen and the engine-room crew remained at their posts and kept up steam for more than an hour, the tide began to rise again, picking up the ship and pushing it farther up the beach with each succeeding wave. "Haul the fires," ordered Chief Engineer Olsen. Shortly after the men stopped the engines, the fastenings of the massive starboard boilers gave way, and the boilers drifted across the sloping boiler-room floor, lodging on the port side. "Everyone on deck now!" ordered Olsen, as water poured down the engine-room hatches.

Ensign Young went below to search for signals and returned with two boxes of Coston lights and an armful of rockets. He sent up five rockets and burned more than a hundred of the lights but could see no response from shore.

Meanwhile, Patti Tillett, a young girl living with her stepfather at a fish camp near Nags Head, was the first to hear the boom of Ensign Young's rockets as she prepared breakfast for her stepfather around 5:00 a.m. When she woke him and told him about the rockets, he told her it was just her imagination and turned over and went back to sleep. Tillett ran outside just as fisherman Evan O'Neal approached on his way to the sound landing, for he, too, had heard the rockets and seen the lights of the unknown ship as she drifted and was pounded along the outer edge of the bar. "Mr. O'Neal, you have to gather some men and go for the beach apparatus," Tillet pleaded.

"Patti, you know there are no men in the station, and we dare not break in," he replied.

Ensign Young, after firing off all the Coston lights and rockets, returned to the poop deck for further orders from the captain. By this time, the *Huron* lay on her port side, bilged, her broadsides inclined about ten degrees with seas breaking over her. "All hands go forward as quickly as possible," ordered one of the officers. As Young passed the cabin door of Lieutenant French, the officer said, "Hurry, we must go quick." Young grabbed hold of the Gatling gun when suddenly a heavy wave washed him and five others down to leeward, temporarily sheltering them from the wind. Young got caught in the bag of the sail and hurt both legs against the gaff, but worked himself forward and succeeded in getting on the topgallant forecastle. The sea finally swallowed the others.

As the tide rose, the stern of the ship became almost submerged. The faint light of dawn appeared in the east as the *Huron*'s surviving sailors clung to halyards, spars, and rigging over the forward part of the ship. Over fifty crowded onto the upper side of the topgallant forecastle with Ensign Young. Some had on life preservers. The bitter cold pierced their wet clothes, and those with extra clothing shared it with others near them. Lieutenant Conway found a blanket, and he and Ensign Young and two others tried to use it as a shield against the cold wind and spray. It did no good. As they became increasingly fatigued, and the cruel sea grew fiercer in its attack on the wreck, more of them lost their lives to the unrelenting bombardment of wind and water. Nearly every furious wave swept someone overboard, tumbling the helpless victim head over heels like a rag doll before drowning him.

Torrents of water broke through rivet holes and ruptured hull plates. The ship's interior flooded. Men driven from the temporary protection of the inner hull fought to maintain a grip on loose gear, all the while being inundated by the raging sea. Those forced to jump overboard drowned in the surf. Crew members, huddled under the forecastle, withstood the fury of the beating surf until the forecastle itself washed away, taking many of them overboard. Most were so bruised and mangled they couldn't save themselves.

Captain Ryan and the ship's navigator attempted to launch the last lifeboat, but it crashed down on them, capsizing the craft and throwing both men into the water. Neither was seen alive again.

The crew's hopes rose when they saw a moving light off the starboard bow. They gave three cheers in jubilation and in an effort to summon their rescuers. Their hopes fell quickly.

The light they saw belonged to O'Neal and Tillett, who had walked over from Nags Head to the beach to investigate. They heard the screams of the men aboard and could see the men clinging to the rigging. But without lifesaving equipment they had no means to launch a rescue and could only stand by and watch the horrible scene unfold. Frustrated, they turned and went home to have breakfast. It seemed that no one would be coming to the *Huron*'s rescue.

A lifesaving station, one of several recently established along the Outer Banks, stood nearby. Unfortunately, Congress had appropriated meager funds for its operation, so at that time Station Number Seven at Nags Head remained closed, its doors locked. The station keeper was at home on Roanoke Island across the sound, and none of the Nags Head fishermen knew how to use the lifesaving apparatus stored there.

Growing higher and higher, the seas carried executive officer S. A. Simmons over the side twice. Both times he clamored back aboard. Then, as if to show him who was boss, a third surge tossed him from his perch and drowned him. Another large wave, sweeping over the ship, carried away twelve men at one time.

The seas around the wreck continued to climb, swelling

from six to eight feet in height. "We must make an effort to get a line to shore," said Conway.

"I'll do it, sir," replied Young. Realizing that the ship would soon be entirely swamped and that no help was likely to come from shore, Ensign Young called for volunteers to help him launch the one balsa remaining on the littered deck. Amid the wreckage, he and seaman Antonio Williams eventually wrestled the balsa over the side and crawled down into it.

His hands numb from the cold, Young struggled to cut the three-inch line by which they lowered the raft. After Williams took Young's penknife and cut the line, they became entangled in the collapsed rigging. Spars, washed up against the ship by the relentless sea, struck them several times. Young and Williams worked for ten minutes trying to clear the balsa.

As they paddled with pieces of paneling, the balsa then drifted toward the stern of the *Huron,* where heavy surf capsized it. Damaged spars and other wreckage pinned both men underwater and nearly drowned them, but they somehow freed themselves and grasped the raft. They remained in the water and tried to swim and simultaneously steer the balsa to avoid its turning over again, but another large swell tossed them a second time.

Ensign Young captured the raft and pushed it toward Williams, who had been thrown about ten feet by the wave. Williams pulled himself into the raft and stood up, desperately looking for a point of reference. He saw what he thought were the masts of fishing boats in the mist, but they were actually telegraph poles on shore. He and Young began to steer toward them. They capsized twice but miraculously hit the beach about three-quarters of a mile north of the *Huron*.

"Haul the balsa ashore," Young ordered Williams. "We might want to use it to get back to the ship." Young and Williams discovered two other exhausted seamen, alive and lying in the surf, near the place where they landed. They pulled them on shore and rested briefly. Young ran to the first house he saw but found no one in it. He continued down the beach as fast as he could, his legs hurting badly from the battering he received from the ship's spars. The ensign came upon O'Neal and Tillett—and ten or so others standing opposite the wreck—looking at it.

"Where's the nearest lifesaving station?" he asked.

O'Neal replied, "There's one seven miles up the beach and another five miles down the beach."

Just then, Young saw a man on horseback and sent him to the upper station for aid and to telegraph to Washington for assistance. It was now about 7:00 a.m.

"Why isn't the lifesaving cart here?" Young asked.

"The lifesaving crew is on Roanoke Island," O'Neal replied.

"Then why didn't you bring the cart up?"

"It's locked up in the station, and we're afraid to break open the door. Besides, we don't know how to use the apparatus."

"If you come with me, I'll break open the door and get it out." Five of them volunteered to go. "Men seem to be landing further up the beach. The rest of you go and do all you can to save them."

As Young and the men approached the station, he saw a team of horses, which belonged to Sheriff Buckley of Dare

City, coming up the beach. Young broke open the station door, got the Lyle gun lines, broke open the locker, and found powder and shot, which Sheriff Buckley brought up the beach with his team.

By the time they got back to the scene of the wreck at 11:00 a.m., all the *Huron*'s masts had fallen, she was almost submerged, and no one remained alive on board. Of the 138-man crew, only thirty-four had survived. Looking toward the surf, Young saw Lieutenant Conway crawling out of it. Lieutenant French was nowhere to be found.

Nags Head Lifesaving Station Keeper B. F. Meekins, who had been summoned from Roanoke Island, arrived at the scene in early afternoon. He had summoned his crew—T. T. Toler, J. T. Wescott, W. W. Dough, James Howard, Willis Tillett, and Bannister Gray—but by the time they arrived, nothing remained to be done but to search for victims in the surf and care for the survivors.

Sheriff Buckley took the four surviving officers—Ensign Young, Lieutenant Conway, Assistant Engineer R. G. Denig, and Cadet Engineer E. T. Warburton—to his house. The others took the enlisted men to Lifesaving Station Number Seven, where they gave them food, clothing, blankets, and beds. Along with them came a dog, belonging to one of the *Huron*'s officers, that had swum through the churning surf.

Then came the grisly task of searching for the dead that had washed up on the beach. The sheriff patrolled the beach for the rest of the day with his team of horses, and one by one stacked the drowned sailors like cordwood in his wagon. He and his helpers recovered only eight bodies. They could see twenty-five more lashed to the main and mizzen rigging on the starboard side of the vessel.

Survivors—bruised and exhausted, suffering from cold and exposure, some completely naked—stretched out on the beach or searched for their shipmates in the surf. They laid the bodies of several in a neat row on top of a dune.

In the meantime the distress message sent by the United States Signal Service operator at Kitty Hawk to Norfolk and Washington had reached the Navy Department, which telegraphed Baker Brothers, a Norfolk wrecking company, to dispatch their wrecking steamer *B. & J. Baker* to Nags Head. The navy also ordered three of its steamers—*Swatara*, *Powhatan*, and *Fortune*—to the scene.

The *B & J Baker* arrived off the Nags Head beach at 7:45 a.m. on Sunday. The sea remained rough, though the wind had moderated. The wrecking steamer lay off the coast for some time attempting to establish contact with the survivors on shore. Captain E. M. Stoddard of the *Baker* considered it too rough to attempt a landing through the surf at that time. At 3:00 p.m. he ordered a boat lowered over the side. John J. Guthrie, Superintendent of the Sixth Lifesaving District; reporter Henry L. Brooke of the *Norfolk Virginian;* Captain Stoddard and his dog; and six seamen as oarsmen climbed aboard. Once underway the boat seemed to have no trouble making for the beach, until it reached a point about one hundred yards south of the *Huron* and two hundred yards from the shore. There it surmounted a huge wave. A second large breaker rose up behind it, overtook the launch, and hoisted the surfboat broadside, and, catching it on the crest of the waves, threw its bottom upward about ten feet in the air, spilling its passengers into the sea.

Stoddard, Brooke, and a seaman managed to catch hold of the capsized boat and held on until it dragged them through the surf to the beach. Another of the oarsmen managed to swim to shore, and the frightened dog swam back to the *B. & J. Baker*. But Guthrie and four seamen drowned, thus bringing the death toll of the *Huron* incident to 103.

Fortunately for the *Huron* survivors, a naval relief party with supplies and medical assistance had arrived about 1:00 p.m., via the inland canal from Norfolk. Even earlier the small steamer *Bonita* had tied up on the sound side of Nags Head, and its captain offered to take the victims to Norfolk. Late in the afternoon the battered survivors—some walking shoeless, others riding in carts—led by reporter Brooke, seated on a Banker pony and wrapped in an army blanket, crossed over from the ocean side to a wharf on the sound, boarded the *Bonita,* and departed for Norfolk, leaving behind the corpses of many of their comrades. A few of the hardier ones climbed the dunes for one last look at the steamer that, just a short time before, had been their home. Now the sea was reclaiming it with relentless fury.

Ensign Young received a Gold Lifesaving Medal for gallantry and humanity at the scene of the disaster, replacing the one that now lay on the ocean floor.

10

A Ship by Any Other Name

METROPOLIS—1878

Twenty-three-year-old Philadelphian Richard Brooks, an out-of-work bricklayer, had been facing hard times as the new year dawned in 1878. With a wife and child to support, he was becoming desperate. And desperate men do desperate things.

An advertisement for construction workers, paying high wages and all expenses, caught his eye. But there was a hitch—he'd have to leave his family and work in Brazil. He signed on immediately, not realizing that in the following days he'd experience the most horrific event of his life.

Brooks's boss, Thomas Collins, of T. & P. Collins Contractors, who had signed a contract with the Pennsylvania Railroad to build a railroad for the National Bolivian Navigation Company in Brazil, also had a surprise in store. For one of the three ships he had chartered to carry his workers and matériel to Brazil wasn't what he thought she was—and that fact eventually spelled disaster.

Collins's first ship, the *Mercedita,* had already departed Philadelphia by the time Brooks signed on, so the foreman told him that he'd be taking the next ship, the *Metropolis,* set to sail at the end of January. The third ship, the *Richmond,* wasn't due to sail until early February.

Though Collins insisted on inspecting each vessel before its departure, he failed to do a sufficient background check on them. As it turned out, the *Metropolis,* which Collins thought had been launched just six years before, was actually the former U.S. bark-rigged screw-steamer gunboat *Stars and Stripes.* During the Civil War, she served as a temporary flagship under Commander S. C. Rowan in the sounds of eastern North Carolina, during which time she had become stranded on a shoal offshore.

The U.S. Navy decommissioned the *Stars and Stripes* at the end of the Civil War in 1865. On August 10 of that same year, Thomas Watson & Sons of New York bought her at a public auction for thirty thousand dollars. The new owners refitted her to carry passengers and freight and changed her name to *Metropolis.* For five years she ran between New York and Havana. Then in 1870 a company from Boston purchased her. The following year, she changed hands again. Her new owners, M. H. Simpson, C. W. Copeland, and the Lunt Brothers, had the *Metropolis* lengthened and her engines made more efficient at Newburyport, Massachusetts, so that she could sail from New York to ports along the East Coast and in the Caribbean and South America. They also altered her papers to say she had been built in 1872, when, in fact, she was already seventeen years old.

Collins was also unaware that the Atlantic Coast Line Railroad had chartered the *Metropolis* the month before he did to transport cotton from Norfolk, Virginia, to Wilmington,

North Carolina, while the railroad rebuilt one of its bridges. The *Metropolis* had left New York on December 2, 1877, and not one day out developed a serious leak in her engine room. The captain called for help and soon a navy ship arrived to tow the weakened *Metropolis* into port. But even before workers patched her hull, the railroad cancelled its charter. The owners of the *Metropolis* sent her back to New York for repairs. Workers stripped, caulked, and painted her hull, then replaced her shaft. And even though they neglected to replace her hull sheathing, Assistant Inspector Craft signed a certificate declaring her seaworthy.

The *Metropolis*, equipped with additional lifeboats for the voyage to Brazil, steamed to Philadelphia, where stevedores loaded her cargo, and on Monday afternoon, January 28, the railroad workers began coming aboard.

A nervous crowd of mostly Irish men, women, and children packed the Reading Wharf at the foot of Willow Street. Tears streamed down the faces of wives as they hugged their husbands, some for the last time. In the middle of the throng stood Richard Brooks and his wife. The captain ordered last call. The screech of the ship's whistle pierced the air.

Some of the men gave their wives one last hug. Others didn't make it in time and had to go on the next ship. Collins himself decided that he and his wife should wait for the next ship after he saw the crowded quarters aboard the *Metropolis*. Brooks walked up the gangway and at the top, as he turned to wave to his wife for the last time, a lump formed in his throat.

The crowd became so thick near the gangway that some of the laborers couldn't get on board and others who had boarded to say goodbye to friends couldn't get off, so the chief foreman hired them to take the missing laborers' places. In all, the *Metropolis* carried 248 people—215 laborers, twenty salon passengers, including three women, and thirteen crewmen—as she slowly made her way down the Delaware River to the bay on January 29, 1878. Among the women, who some of the crew believed to be bad luck, was Mrs. Harrison, wife of William Harrison, one of the men in charge of the laborers.

Besides its passengers and crew, the ship carried almost a thousand tons of cargo, including 500 tons of iron rails, 250 tons of coal, and 200 tons of supplies. The owners hadn't signed the policy insuring it for $42,000 until two days after the *Metropolis* left Philadelphia.

As the *Metropolis* reached the Delaware breakwater, Captain J. H. Ankers discharged the pilot and headed her into the Atlantic. The sea remained calm throughout the remainder of that day and the next as the ship steamed south.

But by Wednesday morning, the weather worsened and the sea became choppy. By mid-afternoon, waves tossed the ship like a corkscrew. Her wooden hull creaked and groaned, the wind whistled through her rigging in a wild, bone-chilling screech. Many of the passengers spent their time at the rail heaving whatever they had eaten since leaving port.

That evening, a mysterious jarring sound coming from the hold awakened the passengers. When the crew investigated it, they found that the iron rails, which had been stored in piles, had begun to shift as the ship tossed about on the ocean. Suddenly someone shouted, "Fire!" Men ran everywhere—some carrying buckets, others dragging heavy hoses—search-

Her wooden hull creaked and groaned, the wind whistled through her rigging in a wild, bone-chilling screech.

ing for the fire. Then just as suddenly a crew member announced, "False alarm. There's no fire." It seems that someone had mistaken steam, escaping from a broken pipe, as smoke, setting off the brief panic. But many of the laborers had been too seasick to bother getting up.

Everyone thought the only thing they had to worry about was trying to keep from heaving as the ship tossed in the rolling sea. But down below, First Engineer Jake Mitteager was having a hard time keeping the ship's engines running steadily. Leaving the engine room in charge of an assistant, he made his way aft and soon discovered a leak near the rudder post, which he promptly reported to Chief Engineer Joseph Lovell, who immediately called upon the ship's carpenter. But the wood in that part of the hull was so rotten that the water just seeped through. Lowell ran to tell the captain. "Cap'n, we've a bad leak in the aft hold, and we'll never make our destination in this condition."

By the time the captain reacted, the water, pouring in quickly, was already four feet deep in the hold. Captain J. H. Anker turned his ship toward the Virginia Capes. "All hands to the pumps!" he shouted. "And keep that bilge pump engine running full time."

"And let's get some men to toss some of the coal from the bunkers overboard to lighten our load," he added. To help with this process, Captain Ankers consulted with Paul J. White, who was in charge of the workmen aboard, to see if he could get some of the laborers to help pass buckets up to the deck. Several passengers, awakened by all the commotion, volunteered to help.

"All passengers report to the main cabin," announced First Mate Charlie Dickman. As they arrived he commanded, "Get the seasick ones out of those berths and then put the berths in the corner." Several removed the hatches and lowered themselves into the hold.

The First Mate ordered the others to form a bucket brigade to transfer the coal from the storage bunkers to the main deck, where others threw it overboard. The men labored until past midnight, throwing over an estimated fifty tons of coal until the load had been sufficiently lightened to enable the pump to gain on the water.

Exhausted from hauling bucket after bucket of coal, Brooks and the other laborers welcomed Dickman's call to stop. But no sooner had they stopped than the iron rails shifted again, opening the seams in the *Metropolis's* hull. The water poured in faster, putting a strain on the already overworked pump until it, too, died. Again, Brooks and the others formed a bucket brigade, this time to bail out the water. However, their valiant efforts were in vain as the ship gradually filled.

As the water rose in the hold, Mitteager found it harder and harder to keep the fires burning. Lovell suggested he break open a barrel of tallow and add it to the fires. For a while, this worked.

By this time, the sea churned and foamed. Without warning, a mighty wave hit the *Metropolis* broadside, carrying away seven of her lifeboats, smokestack, steam whistle, skylight, most of the gangway, engine-room ventilators, the main starboard saloon, and the aft mainsail. The galley stove toppled over, crushing the assistant steward beneath it. Tables overturned in the officers' dining saloon. The force of the water tore off the doors of the forward saloon, and a flood of water engulfed the cabin. The rush of water threw Mrs. Harrison against a bulkhead, causing her serious injury.

The ship went dark as the heavy seas drowned out the gaslights. One of the passengers gave Lovell a lantern so that he could check on the boiler room. "The fireroom's full of water, sir. The men are afraid to go down below," shouted Mitteager.

"We've got to keep up the steam," ordered Lovell. "It's the only way to save the ship. Throw another barrel of tallow in the furnaces and find any wood on the ship that will burn."

A howling snowstorm engulfed the besieged ship. The freezing cold and constant barrage of water numbed everyone. Some crew members passed out life preservers to anxious passengers while others tried valiantly to plug the leaks in the hull. Those who weren't too sick joined the bucket brigade, passing water-filled buckets from one to the other and out the hatchways.

Through the snow, Captain Ankers spotted a far-off light from a lighthouse to the west.

"Set the remaining sails and head her toward shore," he ordered, realizing his vessel couldn't stay afloat for long. The force of a full gale blew the ship along helplessly. As long as the engines held out, the captain had some control, but, despite the frantic attempts of the bucket brigade, the water finally drowned out the boiler fires.

As dawn broke on that Thursday morning, the *Metropolis* foundered in the turbulent sea with breakers dead ahead. With the steam whistle and all but one of her lifeboats washed overboard, and only part of her sails intact, she had little chance against the power of Mother Nature.

At 6:45 a.m. the ship struck the beach headfirst, but because of all the water she had taken on she couldn't sail over the shoals to reach the shallower depths; she was left stranded one hundred yards from the pounding breakers.

Many of the passengers rushed to the deck, but as the powerful sea broke over the ship it swept them into the icy waters. Though they cried for help, no one could save them.

The sea swept away the rear part of the hurricane deck. Those who had sought refuge there quickly scrambled up the

fore-rigging and top forecastle to escape being swept overboard. Some jumped into the roiling sea to attempt to swim
for shore. A violent wave washed Mrs. Myers, the wife of one
of the foremen, out of the pilot house and smack into a rail,
knocking her unconscious. Before her husband could help her,
she drowned. In desperation, he jumped overboard and disappeared beneath the waves.

Through the morning's gloomy mist, N. E. K. Jones and
young Jimmy Capps faintly heard the eerie tolling of the
Metropolis's bell as they walked along Currituck Beach on the
Outer Banks. As they reached the shore, Capps, pointing
toward the ocean, exclaimed, "Mr. Jones, yonder's a vessel
ashore, and it looks like there are people on board." The battered hull and lone mast of the *Metropolis* were just barely vis-
ible offshore.

"Run and fetch Swepson Brock," said Jones anxiously.

Capps ran as fast as he could. Nearing Brock's house he
shouted, "Mr. Brock, Mr. Brock, come quick. There's a vessel
ashore . . . and there's people on it!"

Brock quickly saddled his horse and galloped toward
Lifesaving Station Number Four five miles away, passing the
wreck on the way.

Meanwhile, confusion reigned aboard the *Metropolis*. After
striking the outer shoal, the ship had drifted over it into deeper
water, at last coming to a stop a few hundred yards from the
shore. Thinking they were safe at last, the passengers cheered.
But beyond them lay looming frigid waves that had already
swallowed up those who had been washed overboard. The
remaining crew quickly announced, "Every man for himself!"

Some scrambled for the remaining lifejackets while six others launched the only remaining lifeboat. Someone threw a towline to them, but in their haste, they forgot it.

Brooks jumped overboard and, along with First Mate Dickman and a third man, swam for shore. Breathless, they arrived just as the lifeboat landed. Together, the men stumbled up the beach until they spotted a cow, which began to run. After the nine bare-footed men chased the cow for nearly a mile, they came upon the Currituck Beach Lighthouse Club. They banged on the door, and employee William Jones opened it.

"You must help us," Brooks pleaded. "There's been a wreck and there are many more people on board." Jones gave the men some dry clothes and sent a message to John J. Dunton, owner of the club, who notified Lifesaving Station Number Four. By this time, Swepson Brock had reached the station with news of the wreck.

Immediately John G. Chappell, the station keeper, mobilized his surfmen—William Perry, John and Jim Rogers, Nat Gray, Sam Gillett, and fifty-two-year-old sailor Piggott Gilliken. As he mounted the horse behind Brock, he shouted, "Boys, get that cart loaded and follow us down the beach. Piggott, hand me the medicine chest." The surfmen began loading the hand cart with a breeches buoy, tackle, Lyle gun, powder, three shots, line and fake box, and a Merriman lifesaving suit—the equipment they'd need to perform a rescue. As soon as Gilliken handed Chappell the medicine kit, he and Brock were off to the scene of the disaster.

As Chappell and Brock rode along the beach, they saw pieces of wreckage mixed with dead bodies. Chappell thought he heard a woman's moan and stopped to resuscitate her. The woman, already too far gone, was Mrs. Harrison, who had been swept overboard earlier.

By the time they arrived at a place where they could see the *Metropolis,* a group of residents and survivors had gathered. It had been nearly four hours since the ship struck the shoal. They could see passengers and crew desperately holding onto the mast and spar, trying to stay above the crashing sea. Meanwhile, Chappell hurried from body to body, using stimulants in his medicine kit to bring survivors back to life.

Unfortunately, the lifesaving crew had a difficult time pushing the cart in the soft, wet sand. The nearly one-thousand-pound weight of the cart caused it to sink deeper with every step, even though it had five-inch-wide tires to keep it from sinking. The men, some of whom had walked over thirty miles on beach patrols during the stormy night, struggled with the cart until John Dunton came by on his beach pony and offered to hitch it to the cart. Brooks and other survivors followed him on foot and together they managed to push and pull the cart the rest of the way, arriving at the scene shortly after noon. Almost six hours had passed since the wreck before the lifesavers fired the first shot from the Lyle gun.

The ship lay head on relatively close to shore, so firing a line to her shouldn't have been a problem. But fate wasn't with the lifesavers that day. With a loud bang, the Lyle shot its mortar and line toward the *Metropolis.* It sailed skyward over the vessel and fell into the sea before anyone could catch it. The lifesavers hauled the line back in and recoiled it next to the Lyle gun. This time Chappell aimed lower, landing the line across the port fore topsail yardarm. Second Mate Cozens crawled out on the yardarm and secured it. But when he handed it down to the others, it lay over the spar. As they pulled the heavier line with block and tackle aboard, the line chafed against the jibstay, and just as the block and tackle neared the ship the line broke and dropped into the sea.

After hauling the broken line back and splicing it with another piece, the lifesavers prepared for another attempt. But Chappell discovered he had only enough powder for two shots. Even though there was more powder at the station, it was over four miles away. The horses had been sent in opposite directions—one to gather more lifesavers and the other to deliver a message to the telegraph office at Kitty Hawk.

"I've got some powder at my place," chimed in Brock. "Jimmy, run over and fetch it for us." Capps did as Brock instructed and returned shortly with enough powder for a few shots. But, as luck would have it, the lines separated from both shots Chappell fired. Now they had plenty of powder but no more shot.

Without a line connected to the ship, they couldn't rig a breeches buoy to rescue those on board, many of whom had no life preservers. The lifesavers' only recourse was to pull struggling survivors out of the heavy surf as they came ashore.

Back on the ship, those clinging to the rigging realized they would have to either swim ashore or perish. Alone or in groups they plunged overboard, trusting their lives to the treacherous waves. Unfortunately, few even knew how to swim, so their destiny seemed sealed.

Quartermaster James Poland refused to give up. Grasping

a line on deck, he shouted, "I'm going to make a run for shore with this line. Once I get in the water, feed it to me gradually." Then placing the end of the line between his teeth, he jumped into the churning sea. He made some progress, but as the giant waves broke over him, the current carried the line up the beach. Those on board feeding the line to him ran out of it, so Poland let go of the line and swam for the beach on his own.

Suddenly, the mainmast fell with a loud boom, taking with it the remaining section of the main cabin and many survivors. Several men got tangled in the rigging. Rough debris rolled over even those who could swim, drowning them instantly. The current carried others so far out to sea that they perished from exhaustion. The rapidly disintegrating *Metropolis* became a scene of horror as the bow and stern separated and the forecastle parted from the ship.

Chief Engineer Lovell clung to the rigging until the mast fell. Then, turning to the man nearest him, he asked, "Got a chaw of tobacco?" When the passenger gave him some, he chewed it a few times, picked up a cabin door, and jumped overboard. Lovell drifted northward on the door until being pulled from the surf north of the wreck scene. Three men who jumped with him never made it.

Meanwhile, Chappell put on his lifesaving suit and attempted to swim to the wreck with a line, but the strong current forced him back twice.

True to the tradition of the sea, Captain Ankers remained aboard the *Metropolis* until practically nothing remained. After donning his Merriman lifesaving suit, he jumped into the turbulent surf but it tossed him about so that he was unable to help himself. Chappell spotted him and went into the breakers after him, followed by Brock and surfman Gillikin. They grabbed the unconscious captain and pulled him ashore, his ill-fitting suit half full of water.

Every wave brought with it fragments of the wreck, inter-mingled with severely injured, nearly drowned people. With the seven lifesavers in the lead, residents like Brock and Dunton joined in the heroic rescue effort. Survivors who were well enough, like Brooks, also did their share, pulling one after another of the exhausted and freezing people from the surf.

As the day drew to a close, broken timbers and the bodies of the dead littered the beach. Many had been robbed as they lay senseless in the surf. Someone cut the belt off Mrs. Harrison and tore off her underclothing. The lifesavers dug temporary graves for forty-four bodies the next day.

Chappell and his men built bonfires of driftwood to warm the chilled souls carried to them on the backs of the exhausted rescuers. They took some survivors to nearby homes for shel-ter, but others, nearly nude and numbed by the cold, stayed by the fires throughout the night. At first, the death toll seemed to be ninety-eight, but Chappell later lowered it to ninety-one and finally to eighty-five, the official number. Bodies contin-ued to wash up on Currituck Beach for more than a week.

So desperate for work were the surviving laborers that some begged Collins to let them sail for Brazil on the steamer *Richmond*. Most still wore the clothes given to them by the Outer Banks residents. But Richard Brooks had had enough. The horror he experienced aboard the *Metropolis* would remain with him for the rest of his life.

11

The Christmas That Wasn't

CITY OF HOUSTON—1878

New York Harbor bustled on the morning of October 20, 1878. Ships filled the docks as horse-drawn wagons filled with goods tried to make their way through the throngs of people— some passengers, others there to bid bon voyage. One particularly busy ship was the *City of Houston.*

The Civil War had long been over and reconstruction in the South had gotten well underway. There was money to be made in the South and West for those with the courage to go for it. Many of the passengers boarding the ship looked forward to a new life as homesteaders or cattle ranchers in the frontier lands of Texas. Heading for Galveston, this voyage of the *Houston* began like most others, her spacious cabins full of hopeful emigrants and her cargo hold full of general merchandise to supply the needs of the new pioneers.

Crates of railroad wheels, coach springs, Singer sewing machines, iron kettles, grinding wheels, lead shot, parts for lamps, door knobs, tools and hardware, rope, clothes pins, wire, locks and keys, shoes and shoe brushes, patent medicines, and even toothbrushes stood next to those holding more luxurious items like vases, Haviland china, and silver serving pieces and flatware. There were boxes of personal items, too, like spools of thread, straight pins, bolts of cloth for ladies to make into new dresses, felt hats, and men's and ladies' leather boots. And in among the many boxes lay special items—sleigh bells, snuff bottles, marbles, miniature porcelain dogs, and bird-shaped whistles, wooden croquet sets, harmonicas, and china dolls—items that would make perfect Christmas presents for loved ones for the upcoming holiday. Some of the dolls, many of which had been imported from Europe, were special, with bisque or porcelain heads and hand-painted features. Other dolls had their extremities sewn to a sawdust-filled cloth body, an inexpensive variety popular with the new middle class.

Wide-eyed frontier children would also be expecting red rubber balls, wooden farm animals, toy tea sets, bisque animal figures, and lead soldiers on horseback. For toddlers, there were toy tops and alphabet and building blocks, and for babies, rattles and teething rings.

The railroad arrived in Galveston as early as 1860, making the port a gateway to the southwest. By the 1870s, Galveston had grown into a thriving community and was a jumping-off point for wagons transporting goods to remote towns inland.

To service Galveston's increasing needs, C. H. Mallory & Company of New York authorized the construction of the 1,253-ton propeller ship *City of Houston*, the first iron-hulled vessel in its fleet, built at the Reany, Son & Archbold Shipyard in Chester, Pennsylvania, in 1871. Workers outfitted her with two masts and auxiliary sails rigged in barkentine fashion, with three large triangular sails on the mainmast, mizzenmast, and spankermast, plus a foremast with, from top to bottom, sky-sails, royals, topgallants, topsails, and courses—all square sails. She regularly plied the route between New York and Galveston by way of Key West, carrying passengers and freight. Those going to the southern Midwest and Southwest found it easier to take a steamer like the *City of Houston* halfway there, rather than spend weeks riding in a stagecoach over dusty roads filled with bumps and potholes.

Passengers could expect to spend a little over a week on board the ship. The *City of Houston* made the trip in record time, reportedly taking only four days, seven hours, and thirty-six minutes from New York to Key West, a distance of 1,145 miles. Add to that another three days, one hour, and ten minutes from Key West to Galveston—an additional 850 miles—for a total time from port to port of seven days, eight hours, and forty-six minutes.

But the *City of Houston*'s life as an oceangoing steamship was not without its problems. On May 13, 1874, she collided with the tugboat *Tillie C. Jewett* on the Mississippi River, forty-five miles below New Orleans, as she made her way downriver and the tugboat made its way in the opposite direction. The tug sunk soon after the steamship hit it, drowning two of its crewmen. The Steamship Board fined C. H. Andrews, pilot of the *Houston,* $50 and suspended his license for fifteen days and did the same to John T. Davis, master and pilot of the tug.

Though the ship was not badly damaged from the collision, the following March her owners ordered her to return to the shipyard where she had originally been built. There she received a general overhaul, plus an additional fifty feet in length. When she resumed her regular route from New York to Galveston, her tonnage had increased by 257, thus enabling her to carry more cargo to the Texas market.

Just two days out of New York on this October 1878 trip the *City of Houston* ran headlong into a storm that was moving fast up the East Coast. The storm rapidly intensified, with gale-force winds and monstrous waves that shook the ship violently. For her captain, John Stevens, it was like her maiden voyage all over again—only this time the bilge pumps couldn't hold back rising waters inside her hull.

He recalled the vessel's first voyage, which started out on August 12, 1871, on a note of promise and soon turned to near disaster as she fell upon a fierce cyclone in the Straits of Florida, a stretch of water lying between the Florida Keys and Cuba, connecting the Atlantic Ocean with the Gulf of Mexico. There, at the beginning of the Gulf Stream, circular winds of tremendous speed lashed her rigging hard, toppling her foremast while storm-whipped waves tossed the steamer about like a toy boat in a river rapid, causing her boilers to shift off their bedplates and rupturing feed pipes and steam lines, temporarily disabling the vessel.

Now, she faced a similar danger. Water flooded her engine room, dampening the boiler fires. Soon the engine stopped, leaving the ship to helplessly founder broadside in the troughs. By this time it was 2:00 a.m. on October 23.

Captain Stevens ordered his first mate to rouse the passengers from their cabins. As the sleepy passengers gathered below deck, the first mate and a member of the crew handed out life preservers as the captain explained the situation. "Water has flooded the engine room," he said calmly, "putting out the boiler fires. This has left us with no power, thus no control over the ship. Each one of you must put on a life preserver and prepare to abandon ship, should the need arise."

Stevens knew the outlook was bleak, but he didn't want to cause unnecessary alarm. "Prepare the lifeboats!" he ordered. But as he looked out at the churning waters, he realized it would be pure folly to put the ship's passengers, especially women and children, in them. How could he expect them to row to shore in the dark during this storm? Even if they made it alive, how could they survive on that desolate shore?

The *City of Houston* foundered on Frying Pan Shoals near Cape Fear, an area about as desolate as the plains of central Texas. The captain saw only a slim chance for survival.

"Burn the Coston lights from the pilot house," Stevens shouted to one of the crew. In a few moments the red glow from the lights lit the deck, but the sheets of heavy rain all but blotted them out before any nearby vessel could see them.

"She's settling by her stern," reported the first mate. "The water is nearly ten feet deep in the engine room."

As first light came up over the horizon, the lookout shouted, "Ship to leeward, captain!" But the furious winds prevented the little two-masted brig, some ten nautical miles away, from reaching the stranded ship.

As hope of rescue faded, the steamer began to sink by her stern. Captain Stevens knew he had to order the lifeboats launched. Just as the crew began lowering the first boat, the steamship *Margaret,* bound for Fernandina, Florida, on Amelia Island north of Jacksonville, appeared on the horizon. She

Trunks packed with all their worldly possessions sat on the ocean floor.

dashed toward the *City of Houston* full steam ahead.

As the *Margaret* pulled up alongside the sinking ship, her crew began to transfer the *Houston*'s passengers and crew to her deck. An hour later, all were safely aboard the *Margaret*, even though there were heavy seas. Within a couple of days, all those from the *Houston* disembarked at Fernandina.

Within hours the *City of Houston* sank beneath the waves, leaving only her masts showing above the surface. Furniture and boxes, the only things left to mark her existence, bobbed about. Her cargo, destined for stores in Galveston, had been valued at $150,000. But the tragedy of it all was that her passengers lost their personal belongings. And for some, it was all they had, for they had uprooted themselves and were heading to a new life in Texas. Now trunks packed with all their worldly possessions sat on the ocean floor.

Newspapers in 1878 called the wreck "the Christmas that wasn't." Today, the items that were to be presents for children and adults in nineteenth-century Galveston have become gifts for modern collectors, thanks to modern salvaging techniques.

Mysterious Circumstances

M. & E. HENDERSON—1879

A full moon shone on the sands near Cape Hatteras on the evening of November 29, 1879. The weather had been clear and remained so well into the early morning hours of the next day. By daylight, the surf ran heavy all along the beach near New Inlet and a strong southerly current ran near the shore. At 5:20 a.m. surfman Leonidas R. Tillett returned to the Pea Island Lifesaving Station from his first watch beach patrol to the south. A moderate but chilly northeasterly breeze hit him in the face.

As the first rays of sunlight streamed over the blue-gray waters of the Atlantic, he gathered firewood to build a fire in the galley stove, then woke up the black female cook, and finally climbed the stairs to the second floor. As he gazed through his binoculars from the south window, he noticed a hatless man, who at first he thought was a local fisherman, staggering along the shore toward the station. Tillett awakened Station Keeper George C. Daniels and the rest of the surfmen and bolted out the door to meet the poor man. The dark-skinned seaman, exhausted and dripping, mumbled what seemed incoherent words as he collapsed on the sand. As Tillett lifted him in his arms, the stranger whispered, "Captain drowned, masts gone."

The ship that the seaman had sailed on was the three-masted 387-ton schooner *M. & E. Henderson,* which had sailed from Bull River, South Carolina, with a cargo of phosphate rock bound for Baltimore. She carried a crew of seven— her captain, a cook, and two mates, who were all white, and three deckhands, who were Spanish mulattoes. Originally hailing from Philadelphia, the *Henderson* had been built in 1864 in Pleasant Mills, New Jersey, and had seen fifteen years of service. Rot had begun to undermine her wooden hull, and it was more a matter of when, not if, she would begin to have problems.

On the evening of November 29, she had sailed in close to shore north of Cape Hatteras, but wasn't in any danger. Though there was a stiff breeze and sizable surf, the night was clear, so her captain had no cause for concern. But at some point in the early morning hours of November 30, she ran aground near New Inlet and broke apart quickly.

Tillett carried the shipwreck survivor back to the station and told the cook to take care of him. Meanwhile, Station Keeper Daniels and the rest of the crew started down the beach in search of the wreck. In the eerie dawn's early light, about a mile and a quarter south of the Pea Island station, near the north bank of New Inlet, they discovered great heaps of debris in the surf. About three hundred yards offshore, they could see what remained of the *Henderson* rising and falling on the waves. They began their search for bodies among the debris.

As the lifesavers searched for human remains, they met the Stowe brothers—Ira, J. B., and W. A., all fishermen. "We found a survivor floating in the inlet and carried him back to our camp on Jacks Shoal, a small island over yonder in the sound," said Ira. "Then we returned to the beach to look for other survivors."

"May we borrow your boat and check on the man for ourselves?" Keeper Daniels asked. While he and two of his surfmen headed for the island, the remaining Pea Island crewmen began a systematic search of the debris for survivors, turning up nothing.

On the island, Daniels found the shipwrecked seaman well tended to. The Stowes had wrapped him in warm blankets and given him hot coffee, so that now he was out of danger.

As the keeper and his crewmen rowed back to the inlet, they discovered a third survivor crumpled on the sand near the beach. Daniels ordered the two surfmen to go back and see if he could be helped. They found the survivor unconscious and barely breathing, so they picked him up and quickly carried him to their station, tore off his wet clothes, rubbed his limbs to restore circulation to them, and gave him some brandy and hot coffee. The thankful seaman soon recovered enough to be out of danger. Meanwhile, the others found no other victims or bodies.

None of the three rescued sailors, all deckhands, could shed light on the reason for the loss of the *Henderson* or the circumstances surrounding the death of the others since they could hardly speak or understand English. Being dark-skinned and obviously of a different race didn't help the seamen, either,

They began their search for bodies among the debris.

especially in the eyes of the *Henderson*'s owners. Had they been white, yet still foreigners who couldn't speak English, the whole affair would most likely have been dropped. No one would have asked why the ship had stranded, given the clear conditions, and how it happened that only they, its deckhands, had survived. But because of the color of their skin, the owners had arrest warrants sworn out on them. They had them transported to Baltimore, where they were jailed and waited months before their case finally came to trial.

Daniels, in his report, later surmised that the rottenness of the *Henderson*'s hull plus her heavy cargo of phosphate rock, combined with the heavy surf when she struck the bar, caused the wreck. He observed that one of the ship's spars lay about 250 yards offshore, still attached to some parts of her hull, near where she apparently struck and went to pieces. On the shore opposite the wreck lay "parts of her plank-shear, a section of her bow with breast-hooks attached, sections of her deck fast to parts of the beams, and broken masts, where they had been driven in the break up." From the wreck three-quarters of a mile farther south to New Inlet, fragments lay strewn about. Though Daniels noticed a piece of new decking and several sound timbers, it was evident that rot had begun to undermine the ship.

Daniels further surmised that the *Henderson* couldn't have lasted more than an hour in the state that she was in. But besides her general lack of seaworthiness, other suspicious circumstances surrounded the wreck of the *Henderson*. Why had only three deckhands out of a total crew of seven survived? Equally mystifying was the way she ran aground in calm weather. In his investigation into the cause of the wreck, Revenue Cutter Service Lieutenant Charles F. Shoemaker found two possible causes: Either the captain's gross carelessness and mismanagement contributed to the wreck, or she was purposely run aground. The federal authorities began to wonder if a mutiny had occurred on board.

The three sailors stood trial in Baltimore but went free for lack of evidence, thus leaving the wreck of the *M. & E. Henderson* shrouded in mystery.

Shoemaker also investigated Keeper Daniels and some of his crew at the Pea Island station for their questionable performance of duty. He concluded that surfman Tillett should and would have encountered the wreck on the night of November 29 if he had walked his patrol as prescribed. He recommended that Tillett be discharged for neglection of duty. Shoemaker also discovered that Daniels had deliberately falsified his report, claiming credit for rescue efforts he never performed. He called for not only the keeper's immediate dismissal but also recommended that surfman Charles L. Midgett be discharged for his incompetence due to lack of experience.

Though the Lifesaving Service accepted Shoemaker's report, it kept Tillett at his post, although he soon left the station. The investigation into the Pea Island station and subsequent dismissals showed that the level of competency throughout the Lifesaving Service was inconsistent. After the wreck of the *Henderson* and Shoemaker's report of it, the Lifesaving Service required that all station keepers and their crews be held accountable for their actions and that every crewman maintain a high level of performance or risk dismissal.

13

Against the Tide

ANGELA—1883

Many a ship has been reported lost at sea. Many a captain has gone down with his ship. But not Captain Carlo of the 373-ton barkentine *Angela,* bound for Baltimore, Maryland, from Cartagena, Spain, with a load of iron ore in early March of 1883. The coast north of Cape Hatteras had a reputation for fierce storms, especially at that time of year. But it wasn't a storm that plagued the *Angela.* It was a simple leak.

While this may not seem a big problem, in the late nineteenth century, even with all sorts of technological advances, sailing ships were still at the mercy of the sea. Once a ship set sail, communication with shore ended. If she got into trouble, her captain had to deal with it the best way he knew how. This is the reason that so many ships became lost at sea, just another statistic, their crews utterly helpless.

So was the case with the Italian crew aboard the *Angela* as she made her way across the Atlantic toward Baltimore. Her heavy cargo of iron ore caused one of her seams to open a bit, allowing the sea to slowly pour in. Captain Carlo checked the pumps regularly, and they seemed to take care of the problem, at least for a while. But the seepage grew progressively worse as the days dragged on.

Eventually, the seams in the *Angela*'s wooden hull widened so much that water poured in faster than the pumps could remove it. She began to roll about in the ocean, making it hard for Captain Carlo to control her. Plus, the heavy weight of the iron ore made her sink lower and lower into the water. It became obvious to her captain that she wouldn't be able to reach Baltimore.

Captain Carlo had two choices: He and his crew could remain on the ship, heading her due west until they reached land, or they could abandon ship, drifting for days in the ship's yawl until another ship spotted them or they capsized and drowned—or worse yet, until they all went mad from exposure, starvation, or thirst, having been exposed to the relentless sun and forced to drink the salt water. Captain Carlo chose the former, what he thought would be the lesser of two evils.

"*Sento gli interruttori dell'oceano nella distanza* [I hear breakers in the distance]," announced the *Angela*'s lookout during the evening of March 4. But the sky was so pitch black that he couldn't see anything. By midnight, they could easily hear the thunder of the surf.

Suddenly, the *Angela* struck bottom. Then she seemed to move slowly forward. Finally, she stopped. Captain Carlo rushed to look over the side. But as he did so, a huge wave broke over the ship, throwing him onto the deck. The ship rolled as another wave struck her. Then the crew heard a loud crunching noise. As each successive breaker crashed over the ship, the noise got louder.

"*La nave sta rompendosi a parte* [The ship is breaking apart]," said the captain. That's when they all realized the *Angela* was disintegrating beneath them. Jagged holes began to appear where her seams had been. All that Captain Carlo knew was that his ship had run aground somewhere off the East Coast of the United States.

Only vaguely familiar with the East Coast shoreline, Captain Carlo speculated from his charts that perhaps the *Angela* had run aground on a bar in a shallow inlet or that she might be stranded near Diamond Shoals off Cape Hatteras. Without being able to see through the darkness, land might be as close as a few hundred yards or perhaps miles away. But he had precious little time to think about that now. The heavy surf continued, pounding the ship to pieces.

"*Abbandoni la nave* [Abandon ship]!" he ordered his crew. "*Preparisi per lanciare il nottolino* [Prepare to launch the yawl]."

There in the darkness, the nine members of the *Angela's* crew quickly lowered the yawl into the sea. They immediately boarded it, followed by their captain, and shoved off. To avoid being crashed upon unseen rocks or a shallow shoal, they headed for the open ocean. Shortly after leaving the ship, they noticed a bright red light flickering in the distance. They knew this was the international signal for assistance. "*Forse presto saremo salvati* [Perhaps soon we will be rescued]," assured the captain.

As they drifted about on the black sea with only stars to guide them, they heard a shot, then another. Soon the faint purple light of dawn crept over the horizon. And as the dawn matured, Captain Carlo realized that his ship had run aground less than three hundred yards from shore. On that shore he could see a group of men busily setting up some equipment. The shot he and his crew had heard earlier must have been when the men had shot a line over to their ship, not knowing that no one was on board.

So Captain Carlo ordered his crew to row to shore so that they could beach their yawl near the men. But the men, who were actually surfmen from the Paul Gamiels Hill Lifesaving Station, five miles north of Kitty Hawk, waved them back. The lifesavers then held up a large red flag as a warning. But Captain Carlo didn't understand what they meant, so he and his crew tried again. The men—by now shouting, "Go back! Go back!"—waved him off a second time. Undaunted, the determined captain tried again. And again, the lifesavers warned him to stay away.

Since he was unfamiliar with the coastline, Captain Carlo had no way of knowing that the beach was at its steepest at that point nor that high tide was in, making it almost impossible to land his boat through the pounding breakers. But he realized that something must be wrong if the men kept waving him off. He ordered his crew to row north.

They rowed for several miles before they saw a building with a group of men standing on the beach in front of it. What they didn't know was that they had rowed as far as Caffeys Inlet Lifesaving Station. Seeing the frail yawl bobbing in the surf, the lifesavers immediately hauled the lifeboat from their station down to the gradually sloping beach.

The surfmen heaved the boat onto a set of wooden rollers

As they all jumped in and manned the oars, they took on nearly a barrel of sea water, but managed to reach the seamen.

and together pushed it into the still-rough surf. As they all jumped in and manned the oars, they took on nearly a barrel of sea water, but managed to reach the seamen. They carefully transferred five of the Italians to their boat and headed back to shore, returning for the others shortly thereafter.

"*Grazie, grazie per il salvataggio noi* [Thank you, thank you for rescuing us]," said Captain Carlo as he kissed the sand upon landing, then turned to see his ship wallowing in the surf off in the distance. Though none of the shipwreck survivors spoke any English, they managed to convey their gratitude to the lifesavers of the Caffey's Inlet station. For them, the tide had turned, and they lived to sail again.

14

A Cold December Night

Winter had yet to arrive, and the temperature was already dip-
ping below freezing early on December 5, 1885, as the 61-ton
schooner *Nellie Wadsworth* dropped anchor in Hatteras Inlet,
just south of Cape Hatteras. Like so many before him, her captain had decided to wait out the southwest gale winds before
he proceeded through the shallow cut to Pamlico Sound.

The lifesaving crew of Durants Lifesaving Station, three
miles east of Hatteras Inlet, saw the *Wadsworth* soon after she
dropped anchor and watched her closely for the remainder of the
day. After one of the crew noticed that she had drifted in over
the shoals, he notified the others. They launched their surfboat
and paddled out toward the ship, but finding her riding
smoothly in calm water just beyond the beach and seeing no distress signal, they turned around and headed back to shore.

The beach patrolman swung his lantern as he began his
two-mile walk up the beach toward the limits of the station's
coverage area. He had been walking for an hour and at 9:00
p.m. observed the *Wadsworth* still firmly anchored in the inlet.
But when his relief, W. R. Austin, reached the same spot at

1:00 a.m. on December 6, he discovered that the schooner had dragged her anchors and was lying broadside to the beach among the breakers about 120 yards offshore. Austin signaled to the ship's crew with a Coston light, a vivid red flare inserted in a wooden holder that he held high over his head, that the lifesavers were coming. Then he ran up the beach to the station to rouse his fellow surfmen. He burst in the door breathless and excited: "There's a schooner foundering offshore in the breakers."

The station keeper ran up the tower to see if he could spot the wreck, but the night was pitch black. "Haul out the beach apparatus!" he ordered. The surfmen bolted from their bunks into the darkness and cold, and in the clockwork-like fashion learned in their weekly drills, they prepared for the rescue. After placing the Lyle gun, two seventeen-pound shot with attached line, a breeches buoy, several pounds of black powder, and block and tackle in the beach cart, the surfmen harnessed themselves like horses to the heavy cart to haul it to the wreck site. Normally, they'd hitch their beach pony to the cart and lead him, pulling the cart just above the surf line along the beach, but this night they'd have to pull it in the freezing cold as the breakers clawed at their feet, the keeper leading the pony behind them.

By 3:00 a.m. the exhausted lifesavers reached the scene of the wreck. They immediately began setting up and loading the Lyle gun with black powder and one of the balls of shot. Under a cloudy sky, the men worked by lantern light, and even though the schooner had no lights, their first shot toward the stranded ship landed within easy reach of the crew. But the cold so numbed the hands of the five seamen, who had taken precarious refuge in the *Wadsworth*'s main rigging, that they could hardly move the line.

It took them some time, but after the survivors tied off the line, the surfmen tied a block, with a heavier line called a whip threaded through the block, to the shore end of the lighter line. Then they held on to both ends of the whip line and as soon as the survivors pulled the block aboard the vessel and tied it high on a mast, the surfmen began sending the breeches buoy out to the vessel. To bring the stranded sailors to shore they would haul on the other end of the whip line.

But fate worked against the men of the *Wadsworth* that night. Though they managed to get the block and whip line on board, as they finished tying the block to the mast, it suddenly gave way, breaking off just above the block and crashing into the icy sea. Without the means to secure the hawser, on which the breeches buoy rode, to the wreck, the lifesavers improvised and quickly tied several cork life jackets to the end of the whip line and sent them off to the ship, but they became entangled in downed rigging within a few yards of it. George Richardson, one of the crewmen aboard the foundering ship, jumped into the icy water and swam toward the life jackets. And though he reached them, he became so overcome by the cold that he lapsed into unconsciousness before he could untangle them from the debris.

Meanwhile, the lifesavers couldn't see what was happening but knew that something had happened aboard the ship. Realizing that the line had gone limp, they tied their end to the beach pony and drove him high on the beach. They succeeded

They'd hitch their beach pony to the cart and lead him, pulling the cart just above the surf line along the beach.

in releasing the line, then dragged the unconscious Richardson, entangled in the belts and rigging, back through the frigid surf to the shore.

After clearing the line, the surfmen quickly rescued three more members of the *Wadsworth's* crew by dragging them to shore. The fifth and last man lost his grip on the line, and they had to haul him bodily from the surf. As soon as the lifesavers revived both the last seaman and Richardson using artificial respiration, they began the three-mile trek back to the warmth of the station. Richardson, wearing only light clothes and suffering from exposure, begged them to leave him there before closing his eyes and lapsing back into unconsciousness. Soon after, he died.

Each of the surfmen took charge of one of the shipwrecked sailors and together they resumed the long, cold journey to the station.

The four survivors became so exhausted that they were unable to walk and pleaded piteously to be left there on the beach to sleep and rest. The lifesavers knew this would be sheer suicide and forced the limp seamen to continue. At times, they had to carry them on their backs as they walked slowly up the cold, storm-flooded beach. They reached the station at 7:00 a.m. and immediately set to work building a fire, preparing hot food, and providing the chilled sailors with dry clothing. Then they wrapped each in woolen blankets and gave them coffee laced with brandy to drink. They buried Richardson's body not far away.

After several weeks, the seamen regained their strength, having been too ill and weak to get out of their beds. They returned to their homes, leaving their crewmate, George Richardson, to rest forever in an unmarked grave in the sands of Hatteras Island. The *Wadsworth* never reached Pamlico Sound. Her remains lie buried in the shoals on the north side of Hatteras Inlet.

15

Eighty Hours on High

HENRY P. SIMMONS—1889

On the morning of October 16, 1889, Robert Lee Garnett was busy supervising the loading of several tons of phosphate rock aboard the *Henry P. Simmons* at the wharf in Charleston, South Carolina. His burly figure stood out on the deck as he made sure workers stowed the cargo well in the hold of the 650-ton three-masted coastal schooner. He had worked on the ship for a while and had been to sea plenty of times before, so this was all in a day's work for him.

While Garnett and several other crew members took care of loading the cargo, the others readied the ship for her voyage to Baltimore. The captain had not yet arrived but was expected shortly. The *Simmons* was due to set sail the following day.

October 17 dawned bright and sunny with a southerly breeze. "Cast off," ordered the captain. Garnett undid the ropes from the stanchion on the dock and jumped aboard just as the vessel began to slowly make its way toward the open Atlantic.

For five days they sailed over calm seas under warm, sunny

skies until they passed Cape Hatteras, North Carolina, heading toward the entrance to Chesapeake Bay in Virginia. On the morning of October 23, there were few clouds in the sky and the day looked as if it would be a repeat of the previous five. But by noon the wind began to pick up. The *Simmons* shuddered as the wind whistled through her shrouds. By 1:00 p.m., it blew in gusts from the east, buffeting the schooner and setting its sails to flapping frantically. Dark clouds stretched to the horizon as the wind velocity continued to increase until by mid-afternoon it reached gale force.

"Helmsman, head her into the wind," ordered the captain as the crew struggled to keep the sails from ripping from their lines. The canvas shook and thundered. Blocks banged on deck and in the rigging as wind pressed the main topsail back against the mast. By 8:00 p.m., the wind speed had increased to eighty miles an hour, barely above hurricane force. The sea rose and fell in great mountainous swells, plunging the *Simmons* headlong into the deep troughs, causing her to take on lots of water.

Conditions worsened as the night progressed. "Take in the mainsail," shouted the captain. And as hard as they tried, the crew could do nothing against the force of the gale. Wave after wave smacked them as they clung to the ropes. "Lash the helm and take to the rigging," ordered the captain, leaving the schooner at the mercy of the sea and storm.

As they all clambered up the ropes and held on for dear life, the driving rain pelted their faces. Below them, the ship moaned and groaned as the waves beat at her.

At 10:30 p.m., after riding the storm like a bucking

bronco, the men felt a strong jerking motion. The storm had driven their ship ashore on the lower end of Pebble Shoals at the North Carolina–Virginia border.

As she ground to a halt, the ocean literally swallowed her up. Water poured over her decks and down her hatches as the ocean swept away the top of her cabin. Finally, she sank into the wet sand until only her three masts remained above the surface.

The torrential rain continued into the night, limiting visibility. The eight frightened seamen clung to the slippery ropes, unable to tell where they were. They huddled close together, trying their best to shield themselves from the cold rain.

At 3:00 a.m., the steward, exhausted and suffering from hyperthermia, let out a low moan, then released his numbed fingers from the rigging and fell headlong into the roiling sea, which immediately swallowed him up.

When daylight appeared on the horizon, only seven of the original eight crew members remained alive. Buffeted by the wind, soaked to the skin, and shivering, the men could see nothing but churning foam all around them. The rain continued in blowing sheets through which they could barely make out the low, desolate sand dunes of the upper Banks.

Later that morning, the surfmen on patrol from the Wash Woods Lifesaving Station, North Carolina's northernmost, and the False Cape Lifesaving Station, Virginia's southernmost, both spotted the wrecked schooner on their north and south patrols, respectively. They immediately dashed back to their respective stations to notify the keepers of the wreck.

The crew from the Wash Woods station arrived first and

was busy setting up their beach apparatus when the surfmen from False Cape came on the scene. The *Simmons* sat over one thousand yards from shore, a bit too far to fire a line to her. But the men tried. Unfortunately, it barely made it half way. Meanwhile, a huge wave washed over the wrecked schooner, taking the second mate with it. And just after the boom of the cannon filled the air, another wave swept a third sailor off the rigging to his death. Seeing the lifesavers on the shore, Garnett, himself numbed from the cold, saw the line shoot out from the beach, but when it fell far short, his hopes dashed. Now only five survivors remained. But hours later, another fell from his perch into the agitated Atlantic.

Darkness soon enveloped Garnett, the captain, and his mates. Soaked to their skin, hungry, and barely able to hold on much longer, they had to resort to drinking rainwater caught in their outstretched hands. Garnett used his upturned hat as a receptacle to gather enough water to drink.

The dawn of October 25 found the surfmen from the two stations, now joined by those from the Little Island station in Virginia and the Pennys Hill station in North Carolina, preparing to launch a surfboat to row out to the stranded sailors. As they pushed the heavy boat into the breakers, the pounding surf beat it back, nearly turning it end over end.

The keeper of the False Cape station had one of his men go back to the station to send a telegraph message to Norfolk, asking for a tugboat to assist them in the rescue. Though the tug did make it as far as Cape Henry, the angry sea forced it to turn around and return to Norfolk.

Just after noon another crew member let go of his precarious hold and fell from the wreck's rigging into the sea. The lifesavers stood helpless on the beach, watching as the sea claimed his body. As the day drew to a close, they lighted driftwood fires.

Garnett and two other survivors still clung to the rigging as the third night aboard the wreck began.

The following day, the surfmen again tried to launch a surfboat. And again the angry surf forced them back. Two more attempts also ended in failure.

By mid-afternoon, the numbed hands of another seaman let go their tenuous grip, and he tumbled from his precarious perch into the frothy waters and drowned. An hour or so later, one of two remaining survivors lost his hold and vanished into the tempestuous ocean. Now only Robert Lee Garnett remained.

As daylight quickly faded into dusk, the surfmen could see Garnett hanging perilously from the rigging on the *Simmons* a half mile from shore, but they couldn't tell if he was still alive. But when darkness overtook them, the schooner's tall masts vanished into the eerie blackness. They added more wood than ever to the fires, taking turns watching the wreck, hoping that the surviving sailor could see them and hang on until daybreak.

Overnight the wind diminished in speed and shifted to the west. The breakers, which had crashed over Pebble Shoals with extreme force for four nights straight, finally subsided. Keeper Malachi Corbel of the Wash Woods station, anxious to reach the stricken ship, ordered his men to launch their lifeboat before dawn. As he sat in the stern and steered the boat, his crew rowed it out through the surf to a point near the sunken

Robert Lee Garnett held onto the rigging for more than eighty hours, battling thirst and hunger.

vessel. There they waited until the sun rose above the horizon, then rowed in closer to the ship where they found Garnett, barely alive but holding his own and wrapped in a tattered sail, clinging to the rigging. He smiled faintly as they approached. Numbed from the cold, he climbed down slowly from his precarious perch as several of the surfmen reached out to help him into the boat and wrapped a blanket around him.

Robert Lee Garnett had held on to the rigging for over eighty hours battling thirst and hunger. His brute strength and dogged determination proved to be his salvation. But his fellow crewmen aboard the *Simmons* weren't the only ones who lost their lives during that storm that devastated North Carolina's coast on that fateful day in October 1889. Five other ships foundered in the storm, killing a total of twenty-four crew members.

16

Disaster Strikes

The phone rang loudly, awakening Keeper D. M. Pugh of the Gull Shoal Lifesaving Station from a sound sleep during the early morning hours of March 24, 1891. On his way to answer it, he noticed the clock on the wall said 4:40 a.m. Putting the receiver to his ear, he heard the scratchy voice of Keeper Wescott of the Chicamacomico station, "There's been a wreck a mile and a quarter south of here. Get your men and gear and meet us there."

Just ten minutes before, the 1,919-ton schooner-rigged, screw-steamer *Strathairly* had struck a hidden shoal at high tide in dense fog over a quarter mile offshore. As soon as it happened, the loud screech of her steam whistle pierced the thick night air alerting the night patrolman from the Chicamacomico station.

The patrolman immediately burned a Coston light, its brilliant red flame creating a halo all around him. Then he ran back to the station to alert the keeper and crew, setting off a chain of events that would signal one of the most disastrous shipwrecks in Outer Banks history.

At about 4:45 a.m., the patrolman burst through the station door, shouting, "Ship ashore! Ship ashore!" The crew, trained to react on a moment's notice, dressed and gathered their coats, boots, and hats and scrambled to collect the beach apparatus they would need to rescue survivors of the wreck.

Built in 1876 at the R. Dixon & Company Shipyard in Middlesboro, the freighter *Strathairly* hailed from Newcastle, England. Her owner, McIntyre Brothers & Company, had been hired to ship iron ore from Santiago, Cuba, to Baltimore, Maryland. In addition to her captain, she had a crew of twenty-six. Nearly at the end of her voyage, she had run into a dense fog bank off of Cape Hatteras. After striking the shoal, her crew tried to lighten her load, but her captain knew that this would be a futile attempt to get the ship to slide off the submerged sand bar.

"Clear away the leeward lifeboat," ordered the ship's captain. But just as the crew began to lower it over the side, a giant swell hit the *Strathairly*, shifting it and smashing the smaller boat in the process. And before they had time to react, a huge wave swept the boats on the windward side of the ship overboard. Right afterward, the crew thought they heard a gun shot. It was now 5:00 a.m.

"To the rigging, men," the captain shouted, just as another monstrous wave broke over the vessel. Most of the crew went aloft toward the forward part of the ship. The captain, chief engineer, and first mate went aloft aft. Then with a loud grinding noise that seemed to billow up from the bowels of the ship, the *Strathairly* began to break in half.

The winds increased in velocity as dawn arose at 5:30, creating even bigger waves. With a loud crack the mainmast broke and tumbled over the side, dragging the captain, chief engineer, and first mate with it. So tangled were they in the rigging that it immediately pulled them under the frigid water to drown.

Meanwhile, Keeper Wescott arrived on the beach opposite the wreck. It was now 5:40 a.m. The seas were too heavy to launch a surfboat, so his surfmen quickly set up the beach apparatus and prepared to fire a line to the stranded sailors. Each man was keenly aware of his duties. Three of them began digging a hole in the sand, roughly two feet deep, in which to bury the wooden sand anchor to hold the breeches buoy line taunt.

At the same time, two more removed the fake box from the cart while the keeper and another surfman positioned the Lyle gun. But they couldn't even see the ship through the thick fog. As they readied the Lyle gun, Keeper Pugh showed up with his crew. They, too, set up their beach apparatus, laying out block and tackle and a breeches buoy. Over the roar of the breakers they could hear the frightened cries for help from the stranded men.

With only the voices to guide him, Wescott fired a No. 7 line in their direction. Shooting blind through the dense fog, he had no idea if the line would even reach the ship, but he had to try. At 6:15 a.m., Keeper L. B. Midgett and his crew arrived from the New Inlet station, bringing with them spare lines, extra powder and shot, additional beach apparatus, and a surfboat. Wescott's first shot line fell short of the ship, so his men pulled the line back, rewound it around the pegs in the fake box and began again. They continued shooting lines for the next three hours.

By 10:00 a.m., the fog had begun to lift. As the *Strathairly* slowly appeared through the veil of mist, the lifesavers realized that she had broken in two and that her survivors clung to the rigging on the bow. This time Pugh sent a six-ounce charge with a No. 7 line attached, but it fell short of the ship. The next shot also fell short.

Frustrated, Pugh tried a smaller No. 4–sized line. This landed squarely on the ship's forecastle. As soon as he was sure the seamen had it, one of his men attached a larger No. 9 line to the smaller one. It drew off fine until within a few yards of the wreck when the small line, unable to bear the strain from the strong lateral current, parted and the process had to be started all over again.

Around noon, Albert Smith, one of the stranded seamen, jumped overboard wearing a cork lifebelt. Though he tried desperately to swim to shore, the incessant breakers kept pushing him back. After struggling in the surf he was pulled out, by this time unconscious and nearly dead, by several surfmen. They quickly carried him to the home of ex-keeper John Allen Midgett, who lived nearby.

There they laid him so his head was lower then his feet, then tickled the back of his throat with a feather so that he would vomit the water in his lungs. They put ammonia salts under his nose, then rubbed his limbs until the poor sailor finally came around.

Because there were three station crews and keepers on the scene, the lifesavers lost no time firing off the next shot, this

The patrolman burst through the station door, shouting, "Ship ashore! Ship ashore!"

one carrying a medium-sized No. 7 line. Keeper Midgett used an eight-ounce charge this time, and the shot successfully struck the forward rail, enabling the crewmen on board to grab it. The surfmen then attached an even larger No. 9 line to the smaller one. But the current carried the line so far to port that the sailors hauled it on board very slowly.

Eventually, they attached it to the ship, hopefully assuring success. However, before the whip line and pulley block got more than halfway to the ship, the stout No. 7 line broke, and the surfmen had to begin again. They kept this up—firing a line that would then break or come unattached—until after 3:00 p.m., firing the Lyle gun as fast as the lines could be rewound in the fake box.

"Something must be wrong out there," said Keeper Wescott. "There only seems to be three seamen pulling in the line, and we've already fired off five shots."

Back on the *Strathairly*, only three of the survivors were in any shape to help. Three more had died, including the second engineer and the cook, and the rest, some wearing little clothing, clung to the rigging, their numbed fingers barely able to hang on. Try as they might, they just couldn't hold on to the slippery wet rope.

"Let's send just the whip line to the ship by itself," suggested Keeper Midgett. "Then if it reaches the ship, we can send the block. Once we get both out there, we can figure out how to rig the gear for the rescue." The others agreed.

Shortly after, the lifesavers were able to land a No. 4 line on the ship. To this they had attached a No. 7 line. As the three able seamen began to haul it off, the smaller line snapped in two when the connection with the larger line got within a few feet of the steamer. By this time, high tide was sweeping in. The exhausted surfmen had used every shot line they had and all were by then too wet and heavy. And the surf had become so high and the ship such an unusually long distance from shore that they couldn't row a surfboat to the stranded vessel.

The twenty-one surfmen and keepers from three stations had worked since early morning to connect a line to the ship and every effort had failed. It looked like the lifesavers had come to the end of their limit. Plus darkness would fall soon, limiting their abilities.

At 4:40 p.m., the sixteen remaining sailors on the wreck began shouting to lifesavers, "Please save us!" Then one by one they jumped overboard in a final effort to save themselves by swimming. As fast as they did so, the current swept them south. The surfmen and the nearby residents, many of whom had been watching the scene unfold, quickly ran down the beach. At great personal risk, they waded out into the heavy surf and dragged the men out of the water. Unfortunately, ten had already died by the time they reached shore. Everyone set about to resuscitate them, pulling their arms above their heads, pressing on their stomachs, even holding them upside down, but to no avail.

The six that had made it could barely stand. They said they wouldn't have had the strength to rig a large line on board even if the surfmen had managed to successfully land one to them. Even if the seamen had managed to rig a line, the ship was disintegrating under them. By 5:00 p.m., as they crawled out of the surf, the foremast collapsed, and soon after the steamer itself disappeared beneath the waves.

The surfmen carried one of the sailors, John Northcote, who was near death, to John Allen Midgett's house, where they performed restorative procedures on him, working until after midnight to save his life. They immediately took the other five, suffering from exposure and exhausted by their struggles in the surf, to the Chicamacomico station where they gave them dry clothing and hot coffee laced with brandy. The other surfmen carried the bodies of the ten victims to the station and laid them out on the floor. They never recovered the bodies of the other nine crewmen.

The following day, Midgett took both Northcote and Smith from his house to the station. Meanwhile, the surfmen built simple wooden boxes in which to place the dead and dug graves for them near the station.

Later on the morning of March 26, the Chicamacomico surfmen and local residents gathered with a minister to say prayers at the grave sides of those that didn't make it through the surf. After resting for a time at the station, the lifesavers took the survivors to Elizabeth City, North Carolina, where they boarded a vessel headed for Norfolk, Virginia.

17

The Times They Are A-Changin'

NATHAN ESTERBROOK JR.—1893

While most surfmen patrolled the beaches of North Carolina on foot, surfman L. B. Gray set out on patrol on horseback from the Little Kinnakeet Lifesaving Station, a few miles north of Cape Hatteras, at midnight on February 19, 1893. And though a strong wind blew from the southwest causing the sea to be rougher than normal, the sky was clear. To Gray, it was a routine patrol until he spotted a three-masted schooner, seemingly aground on a sand bar about one thousand feet offshore.

Captain George L. Kelsey had been struggling to navigate the 713-ton schooner the *Nathan Esterbrook Jr.*, her hold filled with thirty-three thousand dollars worth of guano, south along the North Carolina coast when suddenly she struck an outer bar not more than two and a half miles north of the Little Kinnakeet station at 12:40 a.m.

Surfman Gray, scanning the horizon for any sign of trouble, saw the tall masts of the vessel looming in the pitch black night shortly after 1:00 a.m. He immediately dismounted and prepared to light a red Coston flare to assure the ship's crew that help was on the way, but the flare wouldn't ignite. He tried another, then another, with similar results. Grabbing his horse's reins, he quickly mounted, and whipping his horse to a full gallop, sped down the hard-packed sands to the Little Kinnakeet station to summon assistance.

As he approached the station, he pulled on the reins and flew off the horse, running the rest of the way to the station. He stormed through the door and shouted, "Ship ashore, ship ashore!" His fellow surfmen at the station had been sound asleep but his shouts soon woke them. Stumbling around in the darkness, their eyes still half shut, they slipped into their waterproof pants, put on their hip boots, and, running down the stairs, pulled on their waterproof jackets.

"Gray, take one of the men and hitch your horse to the cart," ordered Keeper E. O. Hooper. "You there, load the cart with medical supplies, life belts, extra powder and shot, and don't forget the blankets. The rest of you wheel out the beach apparatus cart." The men scurried around doing what they had been told. But Hooper was a man short. One of his crew was ill at home.

While the six remaining men prepared the equipment, Keeper Hooper telephoned his fellow keepers at the Big Kinnakeet and Gull Shoal stations to ask for their assistance. He then hung up the receiver and ran up the stairs to the lookout tower to burn a Coston light. It was now 1:30 a.m.

The men hitched themselves onto the beach apparatus cart while Hooper took the reins of the horse drawing the supply cart. With their keeper leading the way, they strained to pull the beach apparatus cart along the hard-packed sand just above the surfline. Before long, the crew from the Big Kinnakeet station, leading a pair of government-issue horses, arrived. They hitched their horses to the beach apparatus cart, relieving the Little Kinnakeet crew.

By 3:00 a.m., all arrived at the scene of the wreck. Within minutes, the men had set up the Lyle gun, readied the shot, and Hooper fired it toward the ship, using the vessel's lights to sight it. The shot whizzed through the air, and despite Hooper's keen aim, struck the forestay and bounced off, tossing the line into the sea out of reach of the *Esterbrook*'s crew. "Haul it back, so we can try again," ordered Hooper. The men dragged the line back to the beach, rewound it in the fakebox, loaded a second shot, then Hooper aimed and fired once more. The line again fell short of its target. "Use a lighter line this time," Hooper added. After dragging the line back to shore, the men attached a lighter one, but this time they loaded more powder into the Lyle gun than before. The third shot landed square across the ship's beam, halfway between the mainmast and the foremast.

"Grab hold of that line," ordered Captain Kelsey of the *Esterbrook*. The crew gingerly took hold of the line and hauled it in until they reached the block Hooper had sent to them. "Tie it fast to the mast," said Kelsey, "then hold a lantern high so they can see we've got it secured."

A short time after the shot landed across the *Esterbrook*, Hooper saw the lantern signal. He shouted, "Send them the breeches buoy!" Unfortunately, he had no way of knowing that Kelsey had ordered his men to tie off the line too low on the mast, which could cause the breeches buoy to malfunction. Moments later, members of the *Esterbrook*'s crew helped second mate Charles Clafford into the breeches buoy. After slipping his legs through the two open holes and making sure he was secure, they raised the lantern as a signal for the life-savers to haul him to shore. But just as Hooper's surfmen began tugging on the line, the schooner shifted, leaning toward the direction of the low-hanging line, which slackened even more, plunging Second Mate Clafford into the frigid water. Instead of pulling Clafford to shore high above the water's surface, they dragged the poor seaman through the pounding surf, allowing him to swallow a great deal of water. Flotsam struck him again and again, causing massive internal injuries. Within moments he lost consciousness.

As the lifesavers dragged Clafford's unconscious form onto the sands, they agreed he probably wouldn't make it, but, nevertheless, they put him over the back of one of the horses and rode him up and down the sands until he began to cough water from his lungs. They wrapped him in blankets and sat him by a small fire they had started from driftwood. Soon, Clafford was breathing normally. "There are seven more crew members and the captain still aboard the ship," he said weakly. "But we tied the hawser too low, so there's not enough clearance for the breeches buoy." He added that though grounded, the ship was in fair shape.

Hooper realized that with the hawser tied that low, it would be impossible to use the breeches buoy to rescue the remaining men. Instead, he decided to launch the lifeboat. Standing in the stern, he steered it through the churning surf.

Hooper shouted, "Send them the breeches buoy!"

But the strong wind and current made it hard to control, so he steered the boat back to shore.

By the time Hooper and his men rowed back to shore, the sun had begun to rise above the horizon. As they stood watching the stricken vessel, now listing to port, they could see the crew of the *Esterbrook*. "Take Mr. Clafford back to the station and fetch the life car," ordered Hooper. While some of his men were doing that, he signaled the sailors on board to switch the lines and block to the lee bow to allow for more clearance. As soon as the surfmen arrived back at the scene of the wreck with the life car, they removed the breeches buoy from the hawser and hung the life car in its place, then sent it out to the ship.

The life car made four trips out to the *Esterbrook*, each time carrying two of her crew to safety. From the time they began in the early morning, it took until almost 2:30 p.m. until the last two men arrived safely on the shore. It had taken twenty-three surfmen from three stations twelve hours to rescue eight men. By 3:00 p.m. they had packed up the beach apparatus and headed back to Little Kinnakeet station with the rescued seamen. Meanwhile, Second Mate Clafford had grown increasingly weak from internal bleeding due to his injuries and later that evening, he died. The next morning, the lifesavers of Little Kinnakeet buried him in the sands near the station.

Though in many ways February 20 was like any other day at Little Kinnakeet, this time the surfmen used the telephone to call for assistance from other stations and the new life car to replace the breeches buoy. Technology had come to lifesaving.

18

A Trusting Man

RICHARD S. SPOFFORD—1894

Roger Hawes had faith. Perhaps not in the Almighty but faith in the world around him. But some people are just too trusting, and Hawes was one of those people—he trusted the wrong things at the wrong times. Hawes was the captain of the three-masted centerboard schooner *Richard S. Spofford*, sailing out of Boston.

It was a week or so before Christmas in 1894, and the loading of the stone ballast in the hold of the 488-ton *Spofford* had just been completed. With all hands on board, the captain gave the order to set sail for Darien, Georgia.

The schooner sailed along using every breath of wind, her bow slicing the sea as she made her way south. By the day after Christmas, the ship had sailed past Cape Hatteras. The wind from the southeast had begun to blow harder. Captain Hawes assumed it would shift to a westwardly flow and decided to sail in closer to shore so that his ship wouldn't be blown into the Gulf Stream where he might possibly lose control.

The wind reached gale force and shifted to the west just as he predicted. It blew so strongly that Captain Hawes couldn't turn the *Spofford* about on the offshore tack for fear of losing his mainsail. So he kept his ship as she was, confident that he could reach the sheltered area on the other side of Cape Lookout and anchor there until the storm blew over. Having made the decision to do so, he trusted that it was the right one.

To reduce sideways movement, Hawes ordered the *Spofford*'s centerboard be lowered through her keel. With that done, she drew only twenty feet of water. However, the trusting captain ordered no soundings taken throughout that afternoon and evening. So confident was Hawes that he went to bed as usual and slept until 3:00 a.m., when a premonition of danger woke him. He decided that perhaps he should check the depth of the water. But he was too late.

Instead of being a few miles east of Cape Lookout, the ship was actually only a few miles west of Cape Hatteras. There, Hawes found only shoals and reefs and breakers at the entrance to Ocracoke Inlet, and no deep water or protection from the wind.

The ship bumped along from shoal to shoal in the pitch blackness, tossing the captain and crew about like rag dolls. Finally, the *Spofford*'s centerboard became wedged in the sand, acting like a pivot on which she swung back and forth. The heavy surf soon drove her around broadside, pulling the centerboard violently from the hull. The ship then drifted over the outer bar into calmer water on the other side. "Drop anchors," Captain Hawes shouted, "before she drifts further." The seven crewmen hurriedly dropped both anchors, but the current and wave action dragged the ship closer to shore. She finally came to rest on the inner bar about three hundred yards from the beach. Opposite lay the sleepy Outer Banks village of Ocracoke, North Carolina.

The next morning, several people from the village gathered on the beach, gazing out at the stranded ship. They just stood there and watched, making no effort to rescue the crew, for they didn't have any lifesaving equipment. Neither did they attempt to notify either the lifesaving station located fourteen miles away on the east end of Ocracoke Island or a second one across the Hatteras Inlet at Portsmouth.

Seeing that the people standing on the beach weren't going to help them, the crew of the *Spofford* realized that their lives lay completely in their own hands. Storm-driven waves continued to pound the ship, by now half under water. Just before noon, five crew members launched the schooner's yawl and headed for the beach, leaving Captain Hawes, the steward, and a third crewman on board. But the waves were so rough that the yawl turned over almost as soon as it cleared the ship. Each of the men in it grabbed whatever he could find to hang onto and rode the swells to the inner breakers, where the villagers rescued them.

Earlier in the day, Keeper F. G. Terrell of the Portsmouth station saw the *Spofford,* but he couldn't tell if she was in danger. He decided to gather whatever volunteers he could and started across the inlet in an old rowboat. Unfortunately, Terrell had little equipment to work with since his station was new and not completely equipped. When he reached the scene of the shipwreck, he sent word to the lifesaving station on Ocracoke Island. He tried to muster a crew to row out to the wreck in the ship's yawl, but no one volunteered. The

The next morning, several people from the village gathered on the beach, gazing out at the stranded ship.

Ocracoke lifesavers arrived at 8:00 p.m. By that time, the captain, steward, and the third crewman had sought refuge on the schooner's bowsprit, the only part of the wreck where they could be clear of the breakers. Huddled together, they clung to the bowsprit throughout that cold December night.

The lifesavers from Ocracoke station had to wait until dawn to attempt a rescue. Because of the darkness, it was difficult to see the ship to shoot a line out to it with the Lyle gun. As soon as the first rays of sunlight poked above the horizon, Terrell shot a line over to the ship. Captain Hawes secured it to the mast and shortly thereafter, he found himself being hauled ashore in the breeches buoy. The other crewman soon followed. Unfortunately the steward, suffering from previous injuries and the numbing cold, had died, his body still lashed to the rigging.

Because of the wet and cold and the fourteen-mile walk back to their station, the feet of the Ocracoke lifesavers swelled so much that they couldn't get their boots back on for two days. As soon as the weather had cleared, several of the villagers rowed out to the wreck and removed the steward's dead body, the ship's furniture, and what remained of the rigging, which Captain Hawes sold on the beach before leaving Ocracoke, a disillusioned, despondent, and much less trusting man than ever before.

19

Accomplishing the Impossible

E. S. NEWMAN—1896

The day shone bright as the warm Indian summer sun beat down on the wharf at Providence, Rhode Island. The three-masted schooner *E. S. Newman* tugged at her lines as her crew waited for the last of her cargo, a load of ballast, to be loaded. Captain S. A. Gardiner anxiously paced the deck in anticipation of the arrival of his wife and three-year-old daughter, for they would be sailing with him on this short trip to Norfolk, Virginia.

Hailing from Stonington, Connecticut, the 393-ton schooner began her voyage on a bright October morning, her sails filling as she slowly made her way out of Providence Harbor. For most of her trip, the seas remained calm and the wind steady, blowing from the northwest.

But early on October 10, 1896, the winds began to pick up, creating moderate swells that caused the *Newman* to rise and fall. Her sails flapped in the stiff breeze as the skies above took on a steel-gray look. As the clouds grew thicker and darker, the wind increased in velocity. Rain came in big droplets, pelting the ship and dampening the sails. Soon the deck was awash, the boat rolling and pitching as spray raked the crew like grapeshot. Raging wind and surging seas made it almost impossible for the crew to control the ship.

Foam flew in dense white streaks in the direction of the wind and covered the ocean's surface in great patches. The rolling of the sea became ever heavier. Beyond the ship lay a confused ocean, with waves coming from different directions. The wind picked up their tops and slung them far into the moisture-laden air, creating a constant veil of water that cut visibility to near zero.

The sea hammered the vessel throughout the afternoon, and when night overtook her, the ship entered the eerie world of the eye of a hurricane. But the calm didn't last long, as the winds began blowing just as fiercely from the opposite direction, this time pushing the ship before them. With loud cracks, it tore one after another of the sails from the masts and blew them out over the water. Captain Gardiner couldn't tell where he was. The storm had finally taken control of his ship.

While his wife and daughter sat huddled in his cabin, Gardiner worried that several large waves could bury them, as the ship dove into the next trough only to immediately have to climb out of it to the crest of the next wave. Over and over it dove and climbed, until it seemed like an endless pattern.

The ship drifted all night and through much of the next day—nearly 100 miles southward along the coast of North Carolina before it slammed into a shoal two miles south of the Pea Island Lifesaving Station at 7:00 p.m. and came to an abrupt stop. Holding on for dear life, the crewmen did all they could to keep themselves from being tossed into the roiling sea.

The storm surge was so high that all of Pea Island lay underwater. As Gardiner looked around, he could see nothing through the sheets of rain but the wave-tossed sea. Unknown to him, the *Newman* had drifted within thirty yards of the normal high-water mark before her keel had struck bottom.

"Fire a rocket," he ordered. One of the crew members hurriedly went below to fetch several signal rockets. They lit the fuses. Then with a hiss and a whoosh, followed by the thud of a muffled explosion and a red halo appearing in the moisture-laden atmosphere, they sent a signal of distress to anyone who might be able to see it.

While the captain went to reassure his wife and hold his daughter, Keeper Richard Etheridge of the Pea Island Lifesaving Station discontinued the beach patrols at the start of the next shift at dusk because of the high storm surge caused by the hurricane. Instead, he ordered surfman Theodore Meekins, who was due to start his shift, to climb up into the lookout tower and keep watch from there.

Though Meekins tried to scan the angry ocean in both directions, he had trouble even seeing the station's outbuildings. The rain pounded the tower's windows, blowing in dense sheets and mixing with spray from the breakers. Sand, swirling like snow, added to this mix to make visibility virtually zero. Suddenly, the surfman thought he saw a red glow in the sky to the south. But as quickly as it appeared, it disappeared, leaving Meekins to think his eyes were playing tricks on him.

But just to be sure, he raced down the tower steps, grabbed a Coston light and ran out the door. He lit it and held it above his head until the rain extinguished the flame. "Mr.

Etheridge, come quick!" Meekins yelled, then lit a second light. By now, Keeper Etheridge joined him on the beach. Both men turned toward the south and scanned through the blowing rain and sand of the hurricane.

"Meekins, did you see that?" exclaimed Etheridge.

"Yes, sir, I did," replied Meekins. There was no mistake— both men had seen the red glow of a red light burning in the sky above the beach not very far south. To them, it indicated that a ship was in trouble.

Though a rescue seemed impossible in such bad conditions, Etheridge knew from his twenty years of experience that he had to try. A former slave who fought for the Union Army after his freedom during the Civil War, he roused the rest of his all-black crew—Benjamin Bowser, Dorman Pugh, Lewis Wescott, Stanley Wise, and William Irving—who hitched a pair of mules to the apparatus cart, and headed as fast as he could down the beach. The cart, filled with one of the two 162-pound Lyle guns, plus a sand anchor, fake box, several shots, and reels of line, sank deep into the overly wet sand as they trudged over two miles to the wreck site. The sweeping current of the storm's tidal surge often brought the men and mules to a standstill. But they pushed on.

Once they arrived at the wreck site, Etheridge realized that the high wind prevented them from using the Lyle gun and the crashing surf made it impossible to launch a lifeboat. And with so much water overflowing the beach, his men couldn't dig a hole for the sand anchor that would secure the breeches buoy. Without using the beach apparatus, how else could he save the stranded survivors?

Though circumstances presented Etheridge with a challenge, he devised another plan using two of his men. He chose two of his strongest, Dorman Pugh and Lewis Wescott, and asked, "Do you think you can wade out to the ship tied to lines?" Both men had worked with their keeper long enough to know that he wouldn't have asked if he didn't think it might work.

"We won't know until we try, sir," they replied. The idea was dangerous and might even result in their deaths, but they both knew that it was the only way to help those poor people.

Bowser and Irving tied a heavy line around both of them, firmly lashing them together. Then they wrapped a second line around their wrists, and with Wise and Bowser holding onto it, Pugh and Wescott slowly walked into the churning surf, past the high-water mark and into the deeper waters beyond to the ship. Bending low into the wind, they had to rise to meet each pounding breaker as it rolled toward them. For a time, as the men made their way slowly to the stranded vessel, Etheridge doubted his decision.

Those aboard the ship cheered as they watched the surfmen make their way to them. Captain Gardiner lowered a ladder over the side so when the lifesavers reached the ship they could climb down to them.

When the two lifesavers neared the wreck, Pugh tossed a line aboard the *Newman* using a heaving stick. The captain tied the line around his daughter's waist and handed her into Wescott's arms as he waited on the ladder. As soon he had her safely in his arms, the surfmen on shore pulled on the line and hauled Wescott and the frightened little girl through the roaring

For a time, as the men made their way slowly to the stranded vessel,
Etheridge doubted his decision.

breakers to the beach. Pugh did the same with the captain's wife, then the crew on the beach hauled him to safety.

As soon as the exhausted surfmen reached the beach, Wise and Bowser took their place and repeated the operation, trudging out to the wrecked ship. Each time two returned, two more went out, but each time it took both of them to carry a crew member back after tying a line securely around the fellow, until, at last, they brought the captain back to his wife's waiting arms. In all, Etheridge's men made ten trips to the schooner until all had been rescued.

"Let's get these people back to the station," said Etheridge. After slogging back the two miles to the Pea Island station through boggy sand and water, the lifesavers gave the shipwreck survivors something hot to drink, some food, and warm blankets. The nine of them stayed at the station for three days, all the while glad that they had escaped from sure death.

20

Timbers in the Surf

GEORGE L. FESSENDEN—1898

Lifesaving station keeper L. B. Midgett awoke to gray skies the morning of April 26, 1898. There hadn't been a life lost on a shipwreck along the North Carolina coast for three and a half years.

Though the surfmen of his Chicamacomico station had trained weekly for just such an occurrence, he knew the lack of action had affected them. Without an occasional shipwreck to keep them on their toes, perhaps they might not continue to look as carefully or work as hard. And much like a fire station, there's only so much cleaning and readying of equipment that can be done when not actually fighting fires. Unlike firemen, surfmen must patrol their section of beach in four-hour shifts throughout the day and night. Things were pretty routine until the three-masted schooner *George L. Fessenden* came to anchor four miles off New Inlet on that day.

The 394-ton *Fessenden* hailed from Bridgeton, New Jersey. At twenty-four years old, she had seen better days. On March 30 she set sail from Philadelphia, loaded with 521 tons of stone destined for Southport, North Carolina.

Shortly after leaving Philadelphia, the *Fessenden* put into Hampton Roads near Norfolk, Virginia. Though it's not known why Captain C. B. Norton docked at Norfolk, it more than likely was for some sort of emergency maintenance.

After leaving Norfolk, Captain Norton sailed his ship all the way down the Outer Banks to Cape Lookout, almost to his destination. As he approached the Cape, the wind reared up, quickly reaching gale force, which, in turn, whipped the ocean into a frenzy of giant waves.

Knowing his ship couldn't withstand such pounding, Captain Norton turned and headed for what he thought was a safe haven around Cape Hatteras. He figured the *Fessenden* would be protected from the strong southeast winds. But Mother Nature can be cruel at times.

By the time the *Fessenden* had rounded Cape Hatteras and proceeded northward a bit to relative safety—at least that's what Norton thought—the wind had swung around and a strong nor'easter came roaring in. For the poor, old *Fessenden,* it was like heading straight into the path of a freight train. This proved too much for the failing ship. As dawn rose on the morning of April 26, the vessel's foremast had broken off one-third of its length below its cross spars and her main-topmast had broken off and blown out to sea, along with many of her sails. Norton realized he was fighting a losing battle and headed the *Fessenden* close in to the mouth of New Inlet, where he dropped anchor four weeks after he had set sail from Philadelphia.

Meanwhile, surfman E. S. Midgett of the Chicamacomico station saw the *Fessenden* bearing in toward the coast while on patrol on the morning of April 26. He noticed that she was partially disabled and hurried back to the station to report it. Since the schooner wasn't flying distress-signal flags, Keeper L. B. Midgett flew code flags asking whether the ship needed help. Captain Norton ignored the flags and their call for help.

Though the sun shone brightly and the wind had died down, Keeper Midgett realized that the ship sat in a precarious position should the winds rise again. "Keep a close watch," he ordered his men, "ready the lifesaving gear, and bring it out in case that ship begins to founder."

By the end of the day, the *Fessenden* remained at anchor, riding calmly on the sea. The surfman on night patrol noticed neither any signs of distress nor signals for aid from Captain Norton.

Overnight, the winds picked up and by dawn of April 27, blew harder. Suddenly the surfman on dawn patrol realized the ship had changed its position ever so slightly. An hour later, he noticed she definitely had moved. Looking through his telescope, he no longer could see the *Fessenden*'s anchor cables. Under the strain of the strengthened wind, they had broken, causing her to break anchor and drift headlong for the beach. He ran back toward the station shouting, "Ship ashore! Ship ashore!"

Keeper Midgett had previously alerted the stations on either side of Chicamacomico as a precaution. "Look alive, men," he ordered. "Take the gear about a mile up the beach. I believe that's where she'll hit."

As the men scrambled out to the gear and prepared to haul it up to the point Midgett had indicated, he telephoned New

Inlet and Gull Shoal stations for immediate assistance, then followed his men up the beach.

While the surfmen hurried up the beach to beat the vessel to the spot she was headed for, the ship gained momentum and eventually struck the bar with a severe jolt, throwing Captain Norton overboard. Even after the vessel's anchor cables snapped, he had refused to signal for help. Now the sea claimed him.

The remaining six members of the crew gathered on the forecastle deck. Try as they might, the heavy load of stone in the ship's hull weighted her down onto the shoal. Heavy breakers swept over her deck, forcing the crew out onto the jibboom.

Keeper Midgett fired a shot with his Lyle gun, placing the line almost in the hands of the sailors hanging onto the boom. They had a problem hauling the line aboard because of their precarious position and the strong current sweeping down the coast. Twenty minutes later, as they frantically tried to secure the line, the *Fessenden* groaned loudly and suddenly began to break apart, disintegrating rapidly like a ceramic pot after it hits a hard surface.

Falling debris instantly killed two of the crewmen before they could get off the ship. The current dragged another out to sea, drowning him. The surfmen, each with a heaving line, scattered along the beach and succeeded in dragging the three remaining crewmen from the surf. One was unconscious and appeared dead, but after laying him over a Banker pony and riding him up and down the beach so the bouncing would cause him to vomit the water from his lungs, he came around.

The Fessenden groaned loudly and suddenly began to break apart,
disintegrating rapidly . . .

By the time the lifesaving crew helped the survivors back to the station, nothing remained of the *Fessenden* but rotten timbers strewn in the surf. Seven crewmen, including Captain Norton, lost their lives that day, untimely deaths due to the false sense of security the area north of Cape Hatteras offered an unweary captain seeking safe refuge during a storm.

21

The Midgetts of Hatteras

AARON REPPARD—1899

As dawn broke over the Outer Banks on August 16, 1899, a bank of ominous gray clouds hung just above the horizon, signaling an approaching storm. Summer storms were common along the Banks, but this one would prove different.

By noon, dark gray clouds had moved in and the wind had switched from the southwest to due east, its velocity increasing to nearly fifty miles per hour. The undulating ocean turned into towering swells that looked more like low mountains topped with foam. The Bankers knew the signs. At this time of year, this could only mean one thing—a hurricane. It had been born in the southern oceans off Africa and had swept over the islands of the Caribbean. Puerto Rico had been especially hard hit, and its residents named the storm San Ciriaco, for it had hit the island on that saint's day.

Now the ferocious and slow-moving storm headed northward toward Cape Hatteras. By 4:00 p.m., the wind speed had increased to seventy miles per hour—gale force—whipping the ocean into a frothy frenzy. Surfman William G. Midgett knew all too well what this meant, so he and his fellow lifesavers prepared for the worst.

155

William Midgett came from a long line of Midgetts who had dedicated their lives to saving others. None of the surfmen knew the coast and its currents better than the Midgetts. As the hurricane pressed northward, William Midgett kept a sharper eye out, for it was on his watch that he sighted the first casualty of the storm—the three-masted 459-ton schooner *Aaron Reppard*.

The *Reppard* had sailed out of Philadelphia on August 12, her hold filled with several tons of anthracite coal bound for Savannah, Georgia. Her captain, Osker Wessel, taking note of the change of the wind direction and its increased speed, decided to ride out the storm. He had no idea that one of the worst hurricanes in history would soon engulf the entire North Carolina coast. "Drop anchor," he ordered. "We'll ride this one out." As his crew made ready to lower the anchor, the heavy swells rocked the ship, making it difficult for them to stand.

The anchor hit bottom but the vessel continued to drift toward shore, dragging the anchor through the bottom sands. The *Reppard* drifted closer and closer to shore. Wessel could easily see the breakers pounding the shore as his ship drifted stern-first toward the beach. "Hoist the sails," he shouted. But the wind now blew so hard it was if he had ordered the ship's anchors let go; the *Reppard* was being slowly dragged into the angry surf.

William Midgett, who had reached a point near where the schooner was drifting, watched the scene unfold. He studied the situation as the ship would first make some headway and then drift backward. He knew from the force of the wind and his experience that she didn't have a chance. By now, he had reached the end of his patrol where it met that of the Little Kinnakeet station. He met the surfman from Little Kinnakeet, who had also seen the stricken vessel. "I'm going for help," Midgett shouted above the howling of the wind. "Keep a close watch on her. I'll be back as soon as I can." The other surfman nodded, and Midgett took off back down the beach, at times barely able to advance as the wind buffeted him.

Midgett finally reached Gull Shoal station, breathless and exhausted. He pushed open the door and had to take a moment to catch his breath before uttering, "Ship . . . ashore. . . . Ship . . . ashore!" Keeper Pugh immediately picked up the receiver and telephoned the Little Kinnakeet and Chicama-comico stations. Meanwhile, his crew pulled on their slickers and readied the beach apparatus cart. Those at the other two stations did the same.

Not long afterward, the surfmen from the three stations met on the beach opposite the *Reppard*, which had by now struck the outer bar about seven hundred yards off shore. The scene resembled a scene from a watery *Dante's Inferno*. Extremely high swells produced mountainous waves that crashed so loudly that the men could hardly hear each other speak. Many of the breakers washed completely over the island into Pamlico Sound. Using a sort of pantomime, the lifesavers set up their equipment and prepared to rescue whoever was on the now-foundering ship.

Unknown to them, the *Reppard* had on board her captain, a crew of six, and a passenger named Cummings. As soon as the vessel struck the shoal, all on board headed upward into the rigging. All climbed into the fore-rigging, except crew member Tony Nilsen and passenger Cummings, who headed for the main and mizzen rigging, respectively. From his perch, Cummings could see the long, desolate sand bank, now awash with storm tides, and beyond Pamlico Sound. All seemed hopeless until Nilsen shouted, "There are people on the beach!" The desperate sailors began waving frantically as the lifesavers, who had just arrived, signaled back.

Even though the *Reppard* lay beyond the range of the Lyle gun, Keeper Pugh decided that by the time they got it set up, the ship, slowly drifting toward shore, might be barely within range. He and the other keepers agreed it would be worth a try. They carefully aimed the gun and fired the first shot.

The men clinging to the rigging aboard the schooner watched as the first shot sailed overhead. They watched as the second fell short. And they cheered as the third lodged itself across the head stays. Though the line lay near enough for one of them to grab, the pounding of the waves caused the *Reppard* to jerk so violently with each jolting blow that it was all they could do to hold on.

Suddenly, passenger Cummings lost his grip and fell from the mizzenmast. As he fell through the air, his leg became entrapped in part of the rigging, and he hung upside down. But before he could reach out to grab one of the rigging lines to right himself, the ship rolled and the wind slammed his body hard against the mizzenmast, knocking him unconscious. It continued to do so, bruising his face beyond recognition and beating the life from his body.

As Cummings's body swung in the wind, the *Reppard*

The anchor hit bottom but the vessel continued to drift toward shore, dragging the anchor through the bottom sands.

started to break apart. The mainmast snapped with a loud crack, tossing crewman Nilsen onto the deck. Moments later a huge wave washed him into the sea. Captain Wessel, who had been barely holding onto the foremast, let go and fell into the sea, then started to swim for shore. Realizing that the angry ocean was too much for him, he turned around and started back to the schooner, but before he reached it, his muscles gave out, and he sank beneath the surface.

With another loud crack, the foremast fell, taking with it the five surviving sailors. Four of them bobbed above the water's surface, but the fifth died on impact.

The lifesavers knew that the situation had now become desperate. And desperate times called for desperate measures. "We must go out to get them," shouted Pugh. "There's simply no other way." So four pairs of surfmen each donned cork life vests and tied fifty yards of shot line around their wastes. While one waded into the boiling surf, the other stood steadfast on the beach. Wreckage floated everywhere. One bash with a broken spar, and any of them would be killed instantly. As the seamen struggled to wade through the rough waters toward shore, the surfmen slowly made their way toward them.

Keeper Hooper of Little Kinnakeet insisted on being one of the ones to venture into the surf. But a large piece of timber from the ship struck him, breaking his right leg. The others continued through the quagmire of wreckage-filled breakers. Eventually, they reached the survivors and helped them back to the beach.

Lady Luck was on the side of the three seamen of the *Reppard,* but others weren't so fortunate. By noon on August

17, the wind speed had reached ninety-three miles per hour and in less than an hour climbed to 120. So intense were the winds and so high the tides accompanying San Ciriaco that the surfmen found it impossible to go on patrol. Thus, they didn't discover the wrecks of seven ships caught in the storm until the morning of August 18. Six others vanished at sea. The hurricane lasted for nearly a month, and, according to the United States Weather Bureau, was the worst in the history of Hatteras.

Breakers Ahead

As the steel fired steamer *Virginia* made her way toward Baltimore on May 2, 1900, a stowaway lay undetected in her hold. Little did he know what lay ahead in the next few hours as the ship approached Cape Hatteras, North Carolina.

Built in 1888 at Russell & Company in Glasgow, Scotland, the 2,314-ton freighter, owned by the S. S. Virginia Co, Ltd., of London, England, chugged along in somewhat rough seas. "Leadsman, take a sounding," ordered Captain Charles Samuels. At a little before 3:00 p.m., all seemed well, as the leadsman found no bottom at fifty fathoms. The sea had roughed up overnight although a haze obscured the horizon and Samuels sighted no land. "Helmsman, change course to north by northwest into the wind. We should be heading into the Chesapeake Bay soon and then on to Baltimore." There Samuels expected to deliver the load of iron ore that he had picked up in Daiquiri, Cuba.

Captain Samuels had just sat down to supper. The clock on the wall struck 6:00 p.m. Then came the dreaded cry from the bow lookout, "Breakers ahead!" The captain dashed up to the bridge to take command of the ship.

"Hard to port," he shouted. "Reverse engines." The *Virginia* turned slowly, but before she could slow down, she struck bottom. *How could this be?* he thought. *We still have a ways to go. She must have passed over a lump.* "Full speed ahead," he ordered. But before the chief engineer could open the steam valves, the *Virginia* hit a shoal and stuck. "Reverse engines," Samuels countered. Nothing. "Forward engines." Nothing. Try as he might, he couldn't get the heavy ship to move.

What Samuels didn't know was that he had struck the southeast point of Outer Diamond Shoal, nine miles south by southeast of Cape Hatteras. The sea pounded the ship violently, causing her to begin to fill with water. What he did know was that deep gullies lay between the shoals off the North Carolina coast. And in the *Virginia's* weakened condition, she might slip off the shoal and slide into deeper water, sinking immediately.

"Drop anchors!" the captain shouted as he raced forward to direct the activity. Satisfied that his ship would hold fast, he headed back to the bridge, but before he got there, the *Virginia* groaned and creaked as she broke into three pieces and sank to her rail. He had hardly enough time to leap to the midship section. "All hands abandon ship! Launch the lifeboats," he ordered.

The ship's twenty-four crewmen hurriedly tried to launch the two starboard lifeboats. But as they lowered the larger lifeboat into the water, the ship lurched, smashing it to pieces. They never got the starboard longboat free of its davits. Fifteen of the sailors managed to get the port lifeboat into the water.

Second Mate Moore directed the operation and had fully intended to return to the ship, but the rough sea made that impossible. "Head for the open sea," he ordered the crew, now manning the oars.

As they pulled away, the stowaway, who had snuck up on deck in all the confusion, joined six other crewmen as they lowered the port longboat over the side. Before they could clear the ship, the boat rolled over, drowning six of the men, including the stowaway. One of the four sailors remaining on board the ship tossed the seventh crewman, Chief Mate Wyness, a bow line and the four of them hauled him back onto the *Virginia*. The five, who now remained on board, feared they were in a much worse position than their comrades who had set off on the open sea.

The captain and sailors hastily climbed up the main rigging to escape the ferocious waves now engulfing the ship. The haze had turned to fog. Below them the entire ship lay in three sections. The forecastle itself stood nearly ten feet above the waves. Adding to the horrendous sight was the hissing and foaming of the water as it shot in great plumes over fifteen feet high. Other then the forecastle, nothing appeared above the surface but the *Virginia's* two masts, her funnel, and her bridge, plus a few feet of flagstaff on her stern. All this happened in just over a half hour.

But as darkness fell upon the stranded ship, Samuels wondered how they might create a signal that someone on the shore might see them. *Surely, in this dense fog, no one will know we're here, clinging to the rigging for dear life,* the captain thought. *Even if the fog should lift, how could anyone see the ship through the pitch blackness. We have to burn some sort of signal. But what?*

"Mr. Wyness, aren't there barrels of turpentine and oil stored in the forecastle?" Samuels asked.

"Aye, captain, some thirty gallons," replied Wyness. "But how are we to get it, sir, the sea being as high as it is?"

Stiff and cold from clinging to the rigging, the group of sailors could do nothing more but hope that help might arrive, as they endured the night with only the sounds of the whooshing water from the bowels of the ship and the endless surf to keep them company.

As the sun began to rise, Samuels wondered if perhaps they could reach the forecastle somehow. *If we can reach the forecastle, we would at least have space to stretch our arms and legs,* he thought.

They figured that if they rigged a board seat with some tackle on the rope supporting the main mast, they could slide down, thus lowering themselves onto the bridge. After rigging up the contraption, they each in turn lowered themselves to the bridge. All except the captain, that is. As he descended on the rope, the device became entangled in the rigging and hung in mid-air. The only solution was to cut the ropes used to control the chair's descent. As a result, the jury-rigged boatswain chair slid down nearly forty feet at great speed, causing Samuels to become seriously bruised on landing. Now that they could stretch a bit, they turned their attention to signaling for help.

Even though it was daylight, the thick haze made it impossible to see land. If they couldn't see land, they reasoned that anyone on land couldn't see them. And that would mean that they'd have to spend another frightful night on their wrecked ship. *Our best chance of being seen is to create a signal by burning the oil and turpentine stored in the forecastle,* Captain Samuels thought. Watching the tide throughout the morning, he waited for it to be at its lowest around noon. "I'm going to swim over to the forecastle to create a signal," he said.

"I'm going with you, sir," added chief mate Wyness.

Just as Wyness said that, the captain jumped in and swam forward, all the while hampered by the strong current and continually breaking waves. When he reached the forecastle, he threw a line to the mate and hauled him in. Together they searched for the oil and turpentine to create the signal fire.

The fog continued throughout the day. As night fell upon them, Samuels and Wyness set their signal ablaze. But the rising tide and increased wind made it difficult to keep it lit. At times, the breakers washing over the wreck completely extinguished it. That night, the rains came and heavy downpours further hampered their efforts. But the two determined officers managed to keep their signal fire burning throughout the night. By dawn, they had burned all 30 gallons of oil and turpentine. Now their plight seemed hopeless.

Two nights and one day had passed since the *Virginia* struck the shoal. And under those adverse conditions, Samuels doubted they could hold out much longer.

Meanwhile, the surf patrols of both the Creeds Hill and Cape Hatteras Lifesaving Stations had seen the ship's signal. The Cape Hatteras patrolman had fired off a red rocket, but, unfortunately, the men aboard the *Virginia* couldn't see

The Virginia groaned and creaked as she broke into three pieces and sank to her rail.

through the fog. The keepers of both stations weren't even sure if it was a vessel in distress. They often saw lights near Diamond Shoals, especially on summer nights when ships pass through the sloughs between the Outer and Inner Diamonds. Sometimes fishing boats would also anchor out there.

At 7:00 a.m. on May 4, Keeper Patrick H. Etheridge of the Cape Hatteras station, suspecting that a ship might be in trouble, climbed up into the tower and aimed his telescope toward where the patrolman had seen the ship's signal. Even though the fog was still rather dense, he was able to make out the masts and funnel of the wrecked ship. "Haul out the Monomoy," he ordered as he descended the steps to the lower floor. As his men hauled out the surfboat, he telephoned Keeper Styron of the Creeds Hill Lifesaving Station. "There's a ship ashore," he said. "Head out to Outer Diamond. We'll meet you there."

The surfmen of the Cape Hatteras station rolled out the cumbersome boat carriage from the boat room, dragging it down near the surf. After laying down a frame of rollers, they pushed the boat onto them. Keeper Etheridge watched for the breakers to flatten, then ordered, "Launch her." The men slid the surfboat into the waves, and with split-second timing, jumped and manned the oars. With their backs to sea, the men pulled on the oars in unison. Only Etheridge, standing at the stern, could see where they were going, steering the boat accordingly. It took all his strength to push the heavy steering oar. As soon as they cleared the shallows, they made sail.

Aboard what was left of the *Virginia*, the men had just about given up all hope when suddenly they saw the white sails of the two surfboats coming right toward them. It was 9:00 a.m. and they couldn't believe that anyone would venture out on these high seas to rescue them. They had endured forty-two hours of thirst and hunger, thinking that surely they would die. But when they saw the lifesavers they began to cry tears of joy.

The Creeds Hill surfboat arrived first about a quarter of a mile from the wreck. Keeper Styron, observing the churning sea running over the treacherous shoals, realized it would be folly to attempt a rescue, so he waited for Keeper Etheridge to arrive with his men. As soon as the Cape Hatteras crew arrived on the scene, the two keepers discussed the best way to rescue the stranded seamen without endangering their men or themselves. "I'll take the three from the bridge, and you take the captain and mate from the bow," said Etheridge. Because the surf was so heavy, they had to row around the shoals, approaching the stricken ship safely and getting as near to her as possible. Through skillful maneuvering, both keepers and their crews rescued the shipwreck survivors and, setting sail, made it back to the beach by 5:00 p.m.

Another steamer, the *El Paso*, bound for New Orleans from New York, picked up the fifteen exhausted crewmen drifting in the *Virginia*'s port lifeboat a day after they had left the ship and took them to New Orleans.

23

Derring Do

SARAH D. J. RAWSON—1905

Cold gray light streamed through the window of the Cape Lookout Lifesaving Station on the morning of February 9, 1905. Surfman Kilby Guthrie snuggled under the bedcovers. The air in the room felt cold while his body felt hot and achy. One of the other surfmen in the room sneezed. Yet another coughed with a hoarse, gurgling sound, the sound of someone just getting over a respiratory illness. A bout of influenza had hit most of Cape Lookout's crew. Guthrie, among others, felt weak and not really fit to do anything. From their beds, the surfmen could hear the surf pounding on the shore. Guthrie looked out the window and saw nothing but a gray wall of fog.

Meanwhile, surfman James W. Fulcher stood watch in the station's tower. Visibility hovered at less than a mile as the fog shrouded Lookout Shoals. Keeper William H. Gaskill had climbed up into the tower twice to check with Fulcher on the conditions. As the station clock struck noon, Keeper William H. Gaskill, himself weak from influenza, once again climbed the tower steps, this time to relieve Fulcher. Picking up the telescope, he scanned the fog-enshrouded shoals. At 12:05 p.m., the fog looked like thick gray smoke, billowing above the white-capped breakers. Here and there, he could see a patch of gray-blue ocean. Suddenly, the fog parted, revealing something in the distance. Gaskin couldn't make out what it was at first. But the longer he looked, the more he believed it to be the topmost spars of a sailing ship.

Just as suddenly as it appeared, the apparition vanished as the fog closed in and became a wall of gray once again. All Gaskin could see was the white caps of the foaming breakers as they crashed onto the shore. At first, he thought that maybe his illness and the fog were playing tricks on him. Staring at it for long periods of time often did that. But then he wondered if perhaps what he saw was part of a former shipwreck that the sea had heaved up above the surface of the shoals. After checking his chart and estimating the distance, he believed he had seen a vessel in distress, aground on the fearsome Lookout Shoals.

"Haul out the lifeboat, men," he yelled. Within twenty-five minutes, the half-sick men, several huddled around the station's stove for warmth, had pulled on their oilskin coats and hats, opened the big doors of the boat room, and rolled out the surfboat. The freezing cold air bit their faces and stung their eyes. They summoned whatever strength they had and pulled the boat down to the shore, then shoved it into the tumultuous breakers.

After rowing for four hours, they got close enough to read the name painted in gold on the ship's black hull—the *Sarah D. J. Rawson*. The 292-ton three-masted coastal schooner, out of Camden, Maine, had sailed from Georgetown, South Carolina, with her decks loaded with lumber. Breakers surrounded her as she lay on her starboard side. Her bowsprit, foremast, main topmast, and mizzen-to-stern rigging were nowhere to be seen. Nothing remained on her deck, her deck-houses having been swept away by the overwash. The lumber she had been carrying plus wreckage littered the sea around her. Six frightened men huddled together on her slanted deck, at least what was left of it.

The *Rawson*, with her crew of seven, had run aground on the south side of Lookout Shoals while under short sail in a gale blowing south-southeast at 5:30 a.m. "Take in the sails," ordered her captain. While the crew followed the captain's orders, a wave washed over the deck, sweeping Jacob Hansen, a Norwegian sailor; the captain; and two other sailors overboard. Hansen vanished beneath the rumble and foam. The others clung for dear life to the side of the ship. The sea continued its relentless pounding of the vessel, first carrying away her lifeboat, then sweeping away the fore and aft deckhouses, as well as her load of lumber. "To the rigging," shouted the captain.

Though Keeper Gaskill skillfully guided the lifeboat through the mass of debris to within two hundred yards of the wreck, the turbulent waters and pitching debris forced him back time and time again. As darkness fell, he ordered his coughing and sneezing men to pull the lifeboat to a safe distance and waited.

"Drop anchor," he ordered. "We don't know when she'll break apart, so we're going to have to stay the night." The men pulled their oilskins closer as they endured the cold, damp night.

The incessant waves threatened to swamp their boat at any

moment. Gaskin's experience told him to anchor the lifeboat downwind of the ship so that they could pluck any survivors out of the frigid waters should they fall overboard. But the boat was also in the path of the lumber floating away from the wreck, so pieces of lumber and wreckage constantly banged into them. "Weigh anchor and pull her back five hundred yards to windward," ordered Gaskins. And even though he felt the effects of the cold and fatigue as much as his men, Gaskins encouraged them to stay awake.

Dawn brought only the faintest glimmer of light to the scene. The *Rawson*'s remaining masts had been swept away. The six shipwrecked seamen huddled together on what remained of the wrecked schooner while the nine surfmen did the same in their lifeboat. Neither had food nor water. But at least the sailors weren't sneezing and coughing. Soaking wet and cold, with sore, aching muscles, the lifesavers tried to reach the ship again. And again the surf and debris forced them back. They tried several more times but each time the sea forced them to retreat.

By 7:00 a.m. or so, the wind shifted, causing the waters to calm down somewhat. Gaskin moved his boat to within fifty yards windward of the ship and dropped anchor, and though it wasn't close enough to board her, it was close enough for Walter Yeomans to toss a line on board using a heaving stick. "Tie the line around your waist," Gaskins yelled to the seaman who caught it, "then jump overboard so we can haul you in." The man did as Gaskins instructed and jumped into the cold, churning sea. With what little strength they had left, the surfmen pulled him safely aboard.

Suddenly the fog parted, revealing something in the distance.

As soon as they untied the line from around the drenched and shivering sailor, Yeomans tossed it aboard again, repeating the process until the lifesavers had rescued all six of them. As each survivor came aboard, one of the surfmen would remove his oilskin and wrap it around him, even though he was cold and wet and feeling miserable himself. Now all that remained was to get the rescued survivors back to shore. Summoning what little strength they had, the lifesavers manned the heavy oars and pulled the overloaded boat back the nine miles through the heaving sea to their station.

After twenty-eight hours at sea, the crew of the Cape Lookout station, their limbs aching from sitting so long in the cold, and their cargo of rescued men once more set foot on solid ground at around 5:00 p.m. The *Rawson*'s crew had gone without food or water for nearly two days and had survived because of the way the ship lay. They had been somewhat protected from the cold northwest wind. Joseph L. Lewis and Calupt T. Jarvis built fires in the station stoves while John A. Guthrie prepared hot soup and brewed coffee for themselves and the six sailors. As soon as they gave the survivors some of their dry clothes to wear, wrapped them in blankets, and fed them, the surfmen dragged themselves to their beds, coughing and sneezing all the way.

24

An Unsolved Riddle

CARROLL A. DEERING—1921

Thirty-five-year-old Christopher Columbus Gray, a former navy man living with his wife and son in the village of Buxton, North Carolina, loved to surf-fish and comb the nearby beach. He'd often come out early in the morning when no one was around and cast his line into the surf near Cape Hatteras. On the morning of April 11, 1921, as he cast his line, he saw something shiny at the tide line. On closer examination, he realized it was a bottle with a note in it. When he arrived back at his house, he worked the damp paper out with a small stick and laid it out to dry on the table. As the paper began to dry, a message appeared: *Deering captured by oil burning boat Something like chaser taking off everything Handcuffing crew Crew hiding all over ship no chance to make escape Finder please notify headquarters of Deering.* Gray immediately sent a letter to the U.S. Customs House in Norfolk, Virginia.

The "Deering" referred to in the note was the *Carroll A. Deering,* a five-masted schooner that had appeared mysteriously on Diamond Shoals on the last day of January, seemingly without a crew and all sails furled.

A giant ship at 1,879 tons, she had been built for the G. G. Deering Company, launched in Bath, Maine, in 1919, and named after the owner's youngest son, Carroll Atwood Deering. She had three decks, an oak frame and keel, and pine planking. Mahogany and cypress finished out the captain's quarters and Carolina pine and cypress the other houses on deck. Her masts rose over one hundred feet and carried over six thousand yards of sail.

People and businesses from as far away as Baltimore had plunked down $3,750 to buy a share of her. William M. Merritt, a sea captain from South Portland, Maine, affectionately known as "Hungry Bill" to fellow seamen, held several shares. He'd also be her first master.

On the late spring day of her launch, she flew thirty flags in her top riggings. As workmen removed the wedges that had held the *Deering* in place during her construction, she began to slide ever so slowly down the greased rails into the Kennebec River. Her two huge black anchors stood out in contrast to her gleaming white hull. Eighty-six-year-old Gardiner Deering, who had designed and directed her construction, stood proudly next to Captain Merritt at the helm, watching his sons Harry, Frank, and Carroll. As the *Deering* slid stern-first into the river, Carroll's wife, Annie, scattered carnations and roses from the bow, as she said, "I christen thee *Carroll A. Deering!*" The crowd of onlookers cheered.

First and foremost, the *Deering* was a collier, transporting coal from Newport News, Virginia, to Rio de Janeiro, Brazil, and Buenos Aires, Argentina. In just a year after her launch, she had earned back for her investors over half of their investments.

Arriving from Puerto Rico on July 19, 1921, she awaited a cargo of 3,274 tons of coal from the Pan Handle Coal Company bound for Rio de Janeiro. The ship cleared Hampton Roads, Virginia, on August 26, but just seven days later docked at Lewes, Delaware, a small bay port at the entrance to Delaware Bay.

Before the ship left Norfolk, Captain Merritt told Mr. Pendleton, the ship's supplier, that he hadn't been feeling well. He also confided in him that he didn't like his crew. His previous crew refused to sign on for another voyage, so only his engineer, Herbert Bates and his first mate, son S. E. Merritt, remained on board. Having a difficult time finding new crew members, he turned to Julius Nelson, a Scandinavian agent of the Eastern and Gulf Sailors Association, who found him six Danish sailors—and a Finnish boatswain.

Once in Lewes, fifty-four-year-old Captain Merritt took a room at the Rodney Hotel where he lay in pain from cramps. After trying to shake his ailment for five days, he told his son, "Wire Gardiner Deering and see if he can get Captain Wormell to take over for me." Willis B. Wormell, who had recently retired, was a neighbor of Merritt's in Portland, and a long-time friend.

Wormell, a tall, heavyset man with light wavy hair and a light moustache in his early sixties, left his wife and daughter, Lulu, at Woodfords Station in Portland just in time to make the next Boston and Maine train to Boston. Here he picked up his new first mate, Charles McLellan, then changed to the New York, New Haven, and Hartford line bound for Grand Central Station in New York City.

Her masts rose over one hundred feet and carried over six thousand yards of sail.

Once outside Grand Central Station, Wormell flagged down a taxi. "Pennsylvania Station and step on it." That evening the two men boarded a train headed for Wilmington, Delaware, where they changed to the last train of the night going on down through Delaware to Lewes.

By the time Captain Willis Wormell and First Mate McLellan arrived at the Rodney Hotel in Lewes, it was nearly 8:00 p.m. The hotel had stood as a landmark in Lewes since 1885. Tired and worn, it hosted navy and coast guard personnel as well as tourists, who preferred the grand panorama of the beach and harbor they could see from its second-floor wraparound porch. The following morning, Wormell and McClellan signed on as master and mate of the *Deering*.

Before clearing Rio de Janeiro on December 2, 1920, bound for Norfolk, the *Deering* stopped at several ports in South America. But this time, she sailed without cargo. Not hearing from her owners since she left Norfolk, Captain Wormell decided to dock in Barbados for orders. While there, he met Captain Hugh L. Norton of the schooner *Augusta W. Snow* at the chandler's and agents' offices of Da Costa and Company.

"Where are you headed from Barbados?" asked Captain Norton.

"Hampton Roads," Captain Wormell replied.

"And from there?"

"I don't know. I'll not go any farther with her once I've brought her to Virginia. I'll be going back home to Maine."

Later, Captain Norton met First Mate McLellan at Da Costa's. McClellan begged Norton to take him on as his mate. He quickly said no. That night, Norton overheard McClellan threaten Captain Wormell, saying, "I'll get the captain before we get to Norfolk."

Captain Wormell felt at odds about his crew, so he looked up Captain G. W. Bunker of Calais, Maine, who he thought might be in port. They met on a beach just outside of Bridgetown.

"You look exhausted, my friend," said Bunker.

"I am," said Wormell. "I'm having trouble with my crew. They're the worst I've had as long as I've been a captain."

"Do you think they'll turn on you?"

"Not all of them."

"That's good, but you know it only takes one armed man to stir up trouble."

As they continued walking along the beach, Bunker paused to relight his pipe. "Willis, you need to watch them. You know with Prohibition, smuggling Barbadian rum into the States could give them just the incentive."

Meanwhile, Wormell's first mate got himself thrown in jail on drunk and disorderly charges and the rest of his crew hung out in a tavern near the docks.

On Sunday, January 9, Captain Wormell bailed out McLellan and ordered his crew to weigh anchor. With no further orders, he set sail from Barbados for Hampton Roads.

On January 23, somewhere between 4:00 and 5:00 p.m., the schooner passed Frying Pan Shoals Lightship off the coast of North Carolina on a heading of northeast by east. The deep blue of the late-afternoon sky reflected on the calm surface of the Atlantic. The temperature hovered around sixty degrees. A gentle breeze blew out of the west and southwest. But the weather, always fickle in this area, soon turned nasty.

By Wednesday, January 26, the wind speed had increased to gale force out of the northeast, blowing sheets of rain and mist, at times mixed with snow and hail, across the *Deering*'s decks.

The next day the winds reached fifty miles per hour by noon and sixty by 8:00 p.m. By 10:00 p.m., they blew at seventy-five, hurricane force. But by 6:00 a.m. the following morning, they had decreased to fifty, forty-five by noon, and thirty-five by midnight. The nor'easter seemed to have passed.

The winds steadily decreased in intensity all morning Saturday until they blew at a mild ten miles per hour. Then a dense fog settled in. By 4:30 p.m., the sea over the shoals appeared as smooth as glass and the temperature remained steady at fifty-four degrees.

Suddenly, the Lookout Shoals Lightship's lookout saw a five-masted schooner with all sails unfurled gliding across the sea. James Steel, the lightship's engineer, grabbed his Kodak to catch a photograph of her as she sailed by at four knots. A red-haired man, using a megaphone, hailed him from the ship. "We've lost both anchors and chains in the gale off Frying Pan Shoals—forward word to our owners!"

Thomas Jacobson, the captain of the lightship, grabbed his telescope and scanned the schooner. Things didn't look right to him. He noticed that her crew seemed scattered about the deck with some standing on the quarterdeck, an area normally reserved for the captain. And the person who spoke did so without the formality associated with the captain of a ship. Furthermore, he had red hair and an accent, possibly Scandinavian. But Jacobson couldn't reply to the hailing since the lightship's wireless was out of order.

As the *Deering* passed from sight, a steamer headed south approached the lightship. Captain Jacobson decided to contact them by hand using signal flags and give its captain the message from the *Deering*. But the steamer ignored the signals. Jacobson blew four blasts on the lightship's steam whistle. Again, the steamer ignored them and suddenly turned east. Jacobson looked through his scope to see if he could read the ship's name, but just as he did, several of her crew threw a canvas over her nameplate. The lightship captain knew something was wrong.

At 5:45 p.m. the following day, Captain Henry Johnson, captain of the SS *Lake Elon*, observed a five-masted schooner off his starboard bow. With all her sails set, she seemed to be heading straight for Cape Hatteras. The winds blew moderately from the southwest.

The next time anyone saw the *Carroll A. Deering* was early on the morning of January 31.

Surfman C. P. Brady had the 4:00 to 8:00 a.m. watch at the U.S. Coast Guard's Cape Hatteras Station No. 183. As he stood in the square cupola atop the gabled cedar-shake station looking out over the sea, he could hear the wind whistling under the eaves of the gables. The ten-to-fifteen-mile-per-hour breeze created mists as it blew the foamy tops off the waves breaking three hundred feet from shore in the pale light of dawn. Gulls rode the cold updrafts while circling overhead.

Staring at the endless sea and shore can be mesmerizing, so Brady decided it was time for a cup of coffee. The clock on the wall struck 6:30 a.m. as Brady climbed down from his perch to the station's mess. As he poured steaming coffee from the big enamel pot on the stove into his blue tin enamel cup, the only sounds he heard were the whistling wind and the ticking of the clock.

With cup in hand, Brady climbed back up into the cupola to finish out his watch. He set his cup down and peered through the station's telescope. He slowly scanned the heavy mist over Diamond Shoals. Suddenly, the mists parted, and he thought he saw a five-masted schooner, all sails set, foundering on the shoals.

Scrambling down the stairs, Brady went to Baxter B. Miller, the station keeper, who lay asleep. "Mr. Miller, sir," Brady said softly as he shook him. "Come quick. I think there's a large ship out on Diamond Shoals."

Miller followed Brady to the cupola to take a look for himself. Pulling the telescope to his eye, he peered through it as Brady directed him. There, appearing faintly as the mist parted briefly, lay a giant schooner, appearing and disappearing like a phantom.

"Sir, I don't know where she came from," explained Brady. "When I went down for a cup of coffee, she wasn't there . . . honest."

At 7:15 a.m., Keeper Miller telephoned the Hatteras Inlet, Big Kinnakeet, and Creeds Hill Coast Guard Stations, requesting they stand by. Then he climbed back up into the cupola for another look. This time the ship seemed to float on a cloud of foamy breakers. At 7:30 he phoned each again. "I'm proceeding to the wreck at the southwest point of outer Diamond Shoals. Meet me there."

"Haul out the lifeboat," he ordered, for the ship lay too far from shore to use the beach apparatus. The station's crew quickly rolled out of bed, dressed, and pulled on their slickers. They knew the routine, drilled into them every week. As one of them pulled open the big double doors to the boat room, the others, their hands on the gunwales, pushed the long, white powered boat through the doorway. Then they hitched a large Belgian draft horse to the caisson. Keeper Miller climbed into the boat's bow and, with a snap of the horse's reins, led it down the ramp into the sand toward the water's edge.

They found the ocean a boiling pot of high white foam, so they hauled their boat to the north side of the Cape. But again the high sea held them back, so they turned around and went back to where they began. By this time, the Creeds Hill and Kinnakeet crews had arrived. The wind blew sand and salt spray at them as they unhooked the front wheels and one of the men led the horse away from the boat, letting the bow fall into the surf.

Keeper Miller chose J. C. Gaskill of Creed's Hill and C. R. Hooper of Big Kinnakeet, plus seven others to man the craft. They immediately started rowing through the pounding breakers. Continually, the sea pushed them back, but with the strength of nine men at the oars, they finally managed to get beyond the surf and out to sea.

They had left at 10:00 a.m. and it wasn't until an hour and a half later that they got anywhere near the *Deering*. But the high breakers over the shoals, seemingly coming from many directions at once, forced them to keep their distance. The roar was deafening as the waves crashed into each other twenty-five to fifty feet in the air. The *Deering*, meanwhile, lay in what looked like the surface of a boiling cauldron. "Her crew must have left her in a hurry," shouted Hooper above the din. "They left all sails unfurled and the davit falls hanging where her boats would have hung." There seemed to be no life on board, and at nearly five hundred yards, the heavy spray prevented them from reading the name on her stern. All they noticed was a rope ladder dangling over her side.

Trying several times to get nearer to the foundered ship, Miller finally ordered them to head back to shore. They pulled the boat up onto the beach shortly after 1:00 p.m. Miller knew that at this point there wasn't much they could do since no one seemed to be on board to rescue.

The weather got worse over the next two days. Finally, on February 2, it had lightened up enough for the coast guard cutter *Seminole* to get within three-quarters of a mile of the ship. The cutter's captain observed that the vessel, listing to starboard, seemed to be stuck on the south side of the shoal and not yet damaged from the pounding breakers. Through the mist, he could only make out her home port—Bath, Maine.

Two days later, the coast guard cutter *Manning* arrived from Norfolk, accompanied by the *Rescue*, a tug from the Merritt and Chapman Derrick and Wrecking Company. The *Manning*'s captain could find no debris or any sign of the *Deering*'s lifeboat and dory on the way. By 9:30 a.m., the two boats approached the *Deering*, but received no answer from their hails.

Captain James Carlson of the *Rescue* slowly guided his tug toward the great ship. He could now easily read her name, emblazoned in gold and black on her stern—the *Carroll A. Deering*, Bath, Maine.

Carlson, accompanied by four of his men, left the *Rescue* in its yawl boat, motored over to the *Deering*'s bow on her port side, and boarded her by the rope ladder hanging over her side. She had mired herself so deep into the shoal that her deck stood only six feet above the yawl. They found the schooner's hold filled with water and her seams nearly torn apart. Though Carlson had intended to refloat her, he realized that this would now be impossible.

The *Deering*'s sail canvas rattled loudly in the wind. Two of her topsails had already been shredded by the wind's fierce hammering. Carlson discovered the level of the water in her hold equaled that of the surrounding sea. Checking the forecastle where the crew slept, Carlson and his men found it empty—no belongings of any kind.

"Cap'n, look here," yelled George Snow, one of Carlson's men. When Carlson joined Snow in the ship's galley amidships, he gazed upon an eerie sight. A pot of coffee stood on the stove and on the table lay a pan with slabs of barbecue spareribs alongside a pot of pea soup.

It was as if the crew had been called away hurriedly as they sat down to eat.

As the men worked their way aft, they discovered that someone had obviously tampered with the ship's steering mechanism and broken the ship's wheel on the quarterdeck. Below it, Carlson observed charts scattered about the captain's cabin. His bed lay unmade and his sea chest was gone, as were the *Deering*'s nautical instruments and captain's log.

Among the items salvaged by Carlson's men were the ship's bell, the Bible belonging to Captain Wormell, which Carlson would send to the captain's family, and three starving cats, later adopted by L. K. Smith, the *Rescue*'s steward.

On February 14, fifteen men sailed out to the *Deering* in four small boats. They stripped her of anything that could be sold. Later that day, W. L. Gaskill, Hatteras's wreck commissioner, conducted a public sale on the beach. The residents of nearby Buxton bought the ship's foodstuffs for $44.05. But what the residents really came for were the *Deering*'s furnishings—her lanterns, tables, chairs, mattresses, buckets, brooms, and especially the rope used on the ship. And while the captain's desk sold for $35, the entire ship went for only $25. After deducting advertising costs and commissions, Gardiner Deering received $333.35 for his prize ship, which cost $275,000 to construct and was less than two years old.

Following a severe storm on March 15, the cutter *Seminole* searched the seas off Cape Hatteras for the *Deering*'s wreckage. A little after 5:00 p.m. she discovered a large chunk of the ship, to which her crew attached a line so that the *Seminole* could tow it into a cove. But the strong easterly current swept the craft and its tow eleven miles out to sea overnight.

At 8:15 a.m., the captain of the *Seminole* ordered his crew to set five gun-cotton mines on the wreckage and cast off the line. Around 11:45 a.m., one after another of the dynamite charges exploded with a tremendous bang.

Meanwhile, Christopher Columbus Gray, while again combing the beach near Buxton, heard five loud explosions, thus ending the short life of the *Carroll A. Deering*, but not the mystery surrounding her.

Some thought that perhaps the *Deering*'s crew had mutinied. And even though Captain Wormell confided in his fellow-captain G. W. Bunker in Barbados that he didn't like his crew, there wasn't enough evidence to support this idea. However, it was during Prohibition, so perhaps First Mate

McLellan had made some sort of deal to smuggle in some high-proof Barbadian rum—there were those who would have paid a small fortune for the real thing. And Captain Wormell discovered their plot, so they did away with him. When they reached the shoals, they loaded the boats with their contraband and tried to make a run for Hatteras Inlet. But most likely none of them knew the seas off Hatteras and in the dark they misread the breakers that eventually capsized their boats, pulling them under to drown.

Others believed that the *Deering* fell victim to a storm at sea, which carried her toward Diamond Shoals. After losing control of the vessel, the crew abandoned her. But since the wind had whipped up the waves, the chances of them making shore in those small boats was very unlikely. And if they did abandon the *Deering,* why didn't they trim the sails to help stabilize her?

And that only leaves the note that Christopher Columbus Gray found in a bottle on Buxton Beach. According to the note, pirates had attacked the schooner, capturing its crew. Reports from years before suggested that Russian pirates had been plying the waters off Hatteras, attacking ships in the sea lanes.

Captain Wormell's daughter, Lulu, hopeful that the note might explain what happened to her father, showed it to the relatives of crew members. It seemed that Herbert Bates, the ship's engineer, had written it. But further analysis disproved this theory. In fact, it showed that Gray himself most likely had written the note.

Lawrence Richey, under orders from Herbert Hoover,

then head of the U.S. Department of Commerce, visited Gray. Since Gray had applied to work at Cape Hatteras Light, Richey sent word to Gray that he needed to speak with him about his application. Gray hurried over to the lightkeeper's cottage and found Richey waiting for him.

"Mr. Gray, before we discuss the job, I need to clear up a few things about the *Carroll A. Deering*," said Richey.

"I don't know any more about the *Deering* than I told the FBI," replied Gray.

"I believe you do," said Richey, and with that produced several official documents. "These reports from handwriting experts state that you wrote the note in that bottle. This whole thing was a fraud, originated by you."

Gray knew he had been found out and began to weep. At first, he blamed his cousin. And when Richey chastised him for that, he finally told the truth.

"They wouldn't buy our fish," said Gray sobbing. "The men who work here at the lighthouse would go fish for themselves and not buy from us. And they get a federal salary. We don't. So I planned a scheme to make them look bad so someone would get fired, then there would be an opening . . . and I would get the job. I purposely waited until after they blew up the ship to plant the message in the bottle and report it to U.S. Customs. I figured by that time they couldn't prove otherwise."

Even though Gray had created the false belief that pirates had attacked the *Deering*, he wasn't prosecuted, for there was no law under which he could be punished. And so, the mystery surrounding the *Carroll A. Deering* continues.

25

In Search of Blackbeard's Treasure

QUEEN ANNE'S REVENGE—1718

Veteran shipwreck explorer Mike Daniel had felt excitement before many a dive, but nothing like this. On Thursday, November 21, 1996, he prepared to explore the sea bottom near Beaufort Inlet, North Carolina, in search of the remains of the notorious *Queen Anne's Revenge,* the legendary flagship of Blackbeard the Pirate.

Daniel, along with divers from Intersal, Inc., a salvage and maritime research company based in Boca Raton, Florida, readied their gear. After one last check, they jumped into the Outer Banks' waters 1,200 yards west of Beaufort Inlet and a mile south of Fort Macon. They had conducted extensive magnetometer surveys for the last ten days and today would prove their suppositions right or wrong. As they descended the twenty-two feet to the bottom, they could see parts of anchors and cannon peering through a mound of sand. By the end of the day, they had brought up two iron cannonballs, a lead cannon apron, the brass barrel of a seventeenth-century blunderbuss, a lead sounding weight, and their most prized possession, a brass bell inscribed 1705, which most likely Blackbeard had plundered from another ship.

The size of the anchors indicated to Daniel that this was, indeed, what remained of Blackbeard's flagship, and not his smaller sloop, *Adventure*. Also, the *Revenge* sank intact, unlike other ships along the Banks that usually broke up after grounding in a storm. And the smallest anchor, which Daniel's crew discovered nearly four hundred feet south of the main debris pile, told them that Blackbeard's crew had tried to haul their vessel off the sandbar.

During the decades of the latter seventeenth and early eighteenth centuries, European ships, many from Spain laden with silver and gold, traveled north in the sea lanes along the Outer Banks before heading east. The protected coves along the shore provided hiding places for pirate ships, which sat ready to pounce on the unsuspecting galleons. After offloading the booty, they could make a swift escape back to the safety of the shallow inlets. The pirates also found these same inlets ideal locations for careening their ships, so that their crews could scrape the barnacles off the hull.

Blackbeard was the most infamous of these pirates and a master of psychological warfare. His large, muscular frame enabled him to stand out among his men. A superior sailor and educated leader with a dramatic flair, he prided himself in terrorizing seamen through this brash appearance. Attired in black from head to foot, he wore an assortment of weapons, including a cutlass, dagger, and pistol in his wide leather belt and six more cocked pistols in crossed bandoliers over his hairy chest. To all this he added a bright red cloak that made him resemble the devil himself.

Legend says that when he boarded a ship, he would brandish his cutlass in one hand and hold a cocked pistol in the other. To make himself look even more fierce, he braided his long black beard into small pigtails that he tied with colored bows. Before he made his entrance onto a ship, he would insert slow-burning matches into his beard or behind his ears, sending small puffs of smoke around his face. Blackbeard's reputation preceded him and by the end of 1717, there were few ships' captains that didn't surrender to him without a fight.

Blackbeard began life about 1680 in Bristol, England, as Edward Drummond. He started out as a seaman, but during Queen Anne's War he sailed as a privateer out of Jamaica, attacking French merchant ships. It was at this time that he changed his last name to Teach, although the moniker of Blackbeard came early in his notorious career. After the war ended in 1713, Blackbeard hired on as a crewman on a pirate ship out of New Providence in the Bahamas.

By 1716, he had begun to sail up the eastern coast of North America, eventually settling in Bath Town and Ocracoke Island. To reach Bath Town, ships had to sail through Ocracoke Inlet. Blackbeard found plenty of secluded coves within Pamlico Sound in which to hide his ships. And with his sailing expertise, he had no trouble navigating around the treacherous coastal shoals.

In November of the following year, Blackbeard and his pirates, while sailing off the coast of the island of St. Vincent in the eastern Caribbean, captured the French slave ship

Concorde, en route from Senegal, Africa, to the island of Martinique. At ninety feet long, weighing more than two hundred tons and armed with twenty-six cannon, the strong and fast *Concorde* was a Dutch flute. Blackbeard knew this would be his new ship. He immediately added fourteen additional cannon, bringing the total up to forty, making her more powerful than any British man-of-war. After being rewarded with its command, he renamed her *Queen Anne's Revenge* and flew his unique flag, showing a skeleton holding a dagger in one hand and an hourglass in the other and blood dripping from its heart, from the mainmast.

With a force of up to 150 men, he attacked ships throughout the Caribbean for six months, adding three small captured sloops to his fleet. By the spring of 1718, he had sailed back up the North American coast to Ocracoke. Terrorizing the shipping lanes, he and his men mounted a week-long blockade of Charleston, South Carolina. Taking several hostages, Blackbeard demanded the city give him medical supplies for his men, who perhaps had been stricken by syphilis.

The *Revenge* ran aground on a sandbar twelve days later as she entered Beaufort Inlet. Blackbeard ordered a small anchor dropped some distance from the ship, then had some of the crew try to haul the ship off the bar. But to no avail. He then ordered the sloop *Adventure* to pull alongside and try to tow the *Revenge* off the bar, but since the *Revenge* was much larger than the *Adventure,* it soon became obvious that doing so might damage the other vessel. Blackbeard ordered everything that could be carried be loaded from the *Revenge* to the *Adventure.* Then he shouted, "Sink her!"

He divided his crew between the remaining ships and sailed to Bath Town aboard the *Adventure,* where he surrendered to the royal governor of North Carolina, Charles Eden. Blackbeard swore that he'd quit pirating and would live the life of a respectable gentleman. But before too long, his stash of gold ran out, and he returned to the sea, this time with the idea of encouraging other pirates to settle in Ocracoke. The wealthier residents of coastal North Carolina pleaded with Governor Eden to turn Blackbeard away, but he did nothing. So they went to Governor Alexander Spotswood of Virginia for help.

Spotswood put a price on Blackbeard's head and sent two ships led by Royal Navy Lieutenant Robert Maynard to Ocracoke to capture the pirate. When they arrived on November 21, Maynard, commanding one of the ships, the *Ranger,* discovered Blackbeard's ship, *Adventure,* anchored off Springer's Point.

Maynard stood his ground through the night and as dawn arose the next morning, he approached Blackbeard's ship, only to be driven back by severe cannon fire. He knew his ships and arms weren't a match for the *Adventure,* so he ordered his men below decks. Thinking that he had disabled the King's ship, Blackbeard brought his ship alongside the *Ranger* and boarded her. Maynard came out of hiding in time to fire his pistol at the charging Blackbeard, hitting him in the head. As if invincible, Blackbeard raised his cutlass and continued to fight. They fought until finally Blackbeard cocked his pistol one last time and fell dead at Maynard's feet. Blackbeard had sustained over twenty-five wounds, fighting to the end as if

The Revenge *sank intact, unlike other ships along the Banks that usually broke up after grounding in a storm.*

possessed by the devil. To prove he had indeed killed Blackbeard, Maynard ordered his head be cut off and hung from the *Ranger's* bowsprit by his hair.

It's ironic that Mike Daniel discovered Blackbeard's flagship 278 years minus one day after Blackbeard perished, taking with him the whereabouts of any buried treasure. And while most people think of gold and silver coins as pirate's treasure, in fact, pirates usually took cargo like rum, sugar, or cocoa, which they sold, dividing up the profits, then promptly drinking them away in port taverns. Blackbeard lived life to the fullest and usually spent his share as fast as he made it.

For Daniel and other treasure hunters, the real treasure is a historic one—items from the period that tell about Blackbeard and his times. Cannon, wine bottles, pewter dishes, navigational instruments, and some gold dust are only pieces to the much larger puzzle of the *Queen Anne's Revenge*.

Glossary of Nautical Terms

A

Aboard: On a boat or ship.

Aft: At the rear of the ship.

Aground: Hitting bottom.

Aloft: Above the deck in the rigging.

Alongside: Close beside a ship or dock.

Amidships: In the middle of a ship.

Anchor: A heavy hook that digs into the floor of the ocean to keep a ship from drifting.

Awash: The sea washing over a ship.

B

Bail: To remove water from a ship with a bucket.

Balsa: A light raft made of balsa wood.

Bar: A mound of sand that's close to the water's surface running parallel to the shore.

Bark: A three-masted ship with square rigging on the fore and main masts.

Barkentine: A three-masted ship with square rigging only on the foremast.

Batten down: To secure a ship's hatches.

Beam: The widest part of a ship.

Below: Under the deck.

Berth: A place where a person sleeps.

Bilge: The lowest portion of the inside hull below the waterline.

Bilge pump: A pump used to remove water from inside the hull.

Block: A pulley housed in a case used to gain a mechanical advantage.

Block and tackle: A combination of one or more blocks and the associated rigging used to gain a mechanical advantage.

Boatswain (pronounced BOH-sun): A seaman responsible for repairing the rigging and sails.

Boatswain chair: A board rigged with tackle used to hoist a crewman aloft.

Boom: A horizontal spar attached to the bottom edge of a sail.

Bow: The forward part of a ship.

Bow line: The docking line leading from the bow.

Bowsprit: A spar extending out from the ship's bow used to secure forward or head sails (also called a widow-maker, since seamen often fell to their deaths while tending sails).

Breaker: A wave that approaches the shore.

Breeches buoy: A circular life buoy used by lifesaving crews to rescue persons from wrecked vessels.

Brig: A two-masted vessel with both masts square rigged.

Bulkhead: Below-deck walls inside a ship.

Bulwark: An extension of a ship's side above the deck to prevent persons from washing overboard.

Bunker: A coal storage compartment.

C

Cabin: A compartment for passengers or crewmen.

Canvas: Another word for sail.

Capsize: When a ship turns over.

Captain: The master of a ship.

Cast off: To release lines holding a ship to a mooring.

Chart: A map used to navigate a ship.

Coston light: A vivid red flare inserted in a wooden holder.

Course: A compass heading.

Current: Water moving in a horizontal direction.

Cutter: A sloop with one mast, rigged with a mainsail and two headsails.

D

Davits: Small cranes used for lowering lifeboats.

Dead ahead: Directly ahead.

Deck: A floor of a ship.

Dinghy: A small boat.

Dutch flute: A large eighteenth-century flat-bottom cargo ship that was a favorite with pirates.

E

Ebb: The movement of the tide from high to low out to sea.

F

Fake box: A box used to coil line to be shot out of a Lyle gun.

Fast: To secure one object to another.

Fathom: A maritime measurement of six feet.

Flotsam: Floating debris.

Forecastle or **fo'c'sle** (pronounced *focsil*): The extreme forward compartment of a ship.

Foremast: The mast nearest the bow.

Forward: Toward the bow of a ship.

Founder: When a vessel fills with water and sinks.

Furl: To roll a sail and secure it.

G

Gaff: The spar attached to the top of a sail.

Gale: A strong wind over forty miles per hour.

Galley: The kitchen of a ship.

Gangway: The ramp used as a walkway from dock to ship.

Gear: A term applied to ropes, blocks, tackle, and other equipment.

Gunwale (pronounced *gunnel*): The upper railing of a ship's side.

H

Halyards: The lines used to haul up the sails and booms.

Harbor: A safe anchorage or a place for docking and loading.

Hard over: Turning the ship's wheel as far as possible.

Hatch: An opening for entering below deck.

Heading: The direction in which a vessel's bow points.

Helmsman: The crewman responsible for steering the ship.

Hoist: To raise aloft.

Hold: The space for cargo below the deck of a ship.

Hull: The main body of a ship, not including the deck, mast, or cabin.

Hurricane: A strong tropical revolving storm with winds of seventy-four miles per hour or higher.

Hurricane deck: The upper deck of a steam packet.

J

Jibboom: The spar forward of the bowsprit.

Jibstay: A jib (triangular foresail in front of the foremast) attached to a stay.

K

Keel: The centerline of a ship running fore and aft.

L

Leeward: Downwind.

Life car: A fat, watertight metal cigar-shaped rescue apparatus, capable of holding four persons.

Lines: Ropes used aboard a ship.

List: To lean to one side.

Log: A record of a ship's course and operation.

Lyle gun: A short-barreled cannon used to shoot a projectile attached to a line to a ship.

M

Mainmast: The tallest mast of a ship.

Mainsail: The sail set on the mainmast.

Mast: A wooden pole used to hold up the sails.

Merriman lifesaving suit: A rubber suit, with compartments filled with air, designed by C. S. Merriman for steamship passengers.

Mizzen: The mast aft of a ship's mainmast.

O

Oilskin: Garments treated with linseed oil for waterproofing.

Overboard: Over the side of a ship.

P

Pilot: The person qualified to guide a ship into or out of a harbor.

Pirate: A person who attacks and robs ships at sea.

Pitching: The up-and-down movement of the front of a ship.

Planking: Wooden boards covering the frame of the hull.

Port: The left side of a ship when facing forward.

Q

Quarterdeck: The part of a ship's upper deck near the stern where the captain and officers traditionally stood.

R

Reef: To reduce the size of a sail.

Rigging: The ropes supporting the masts and sails.

Rudder: A fin attached vertically under a ship's stern used for steering.

S

Sail: A piece of cloth that catches the wind and propels a ship.

Salon (or saloon): The main social cabin of a ship.

Schooner: A sailing ship with at least two masts.

Secure: To make fast.

Ship's bells: Every half hour a crewman rings the ship's bell to announce the time, starting at one bell (0030) until eight bells (0400), which indicates the time to change the watch. Then he begins again with one bell to the next eight bells.

Shot: A fourteen-inch, seventeen-pound projectile with an eye bolt for attaching a line, fired from a Lyle gun.

Sloop: A typical single-masted sailboat with a single headsail.

Spar: A pole.

Starboard: The right side of a ship when facing forward.

Stay: A rope from the mast to the bow or stern of a ship, for support of the mast.

Staysail: A sail attached to a stay.

Stern: The back end of a ship.

Surge: A sudden, swelling wave.

T

Tide: The rise and fall of the sea due to the attraction of the sun and moon.

Topgallant forecastle: the section of a square-rigged sailing ship's mast immediately above the topmast.

Topgallant sail: The sail above the topsail on a square-rigged ship.

Topmast: A second section of a square-rigged sailing ship's mast.

Topsail: The topmost sail. On a square-rigged ship, the second or third sail above the mainsail.

Trim: To adjust the sails.

U

Underway: When a ship is moving.

W

Weigh: To haul up.

Wheel: A device used for steering a ship.

Windward: Upwind.

Y

Yard: A horizontal spar that supports a square sail.

Yardarm: The outer part of a ship's yard.

Yawl: a two-masted fore-and-aft-rigged sailing boat with the mizzenmast stepped far aft so that the mizzen boom overhangs the stern.

Additional Resources

Barnett, J. P. *The Lifesaving Guns of David Lyle*. South Bend, IN: South Bend Replicas, 1976.

Berman, Bruce D. *Encyclopedia of American Shipwrecks*. Boston: The Mariners Press, 1972.

Granbarba, Paul. *Surfmen and Lifesavers*. Centerville, MA: Scrimshaw, 1967.

Heyl, Erik. *Early American Steamers*. Buffalo, NY: Erik Heyl, 1969.

Johnson, Robert Erwin. *Guardians of the Sea: History of the United States Coast Guard, 1915 to the Present*. Annapolis, MD: Naval Institute Press, 1987.

Kaplan, H. R. *A Guide to Sunken Ships in American Waters*. Arlington, VA: Compass Publications, 1964.

Lee, Robert E. *Blackbeard the Pirate: A Reappraisal of His Life and Times*. Winston-Salem, NC: J. F. Blair, 1974

MacNeill, Ben Dixon. *The Hatterasman*. Winston-Salem, NC: John F. Blair, 1958.

Paine, Ralph D. *The Book of Buried Treasure—Being a True History of the Gold, Jewels, and Plate of Pirates, Galleons, Etc.* New York, 1911.

Rankin, Hugh F. *The Pirates of North Carolina*. Division of Archives and History, North Carolina Department of Cultural Resources, Raleigh, North Carolina, 1989.

Stick, David. *The Outer Banks of North Carolina, 1584–1958*. Chapel Hill: University of North Carolina Press, 1958.

Whedbee, Charles Harry. *Outer Banks Mysteries & Seaside Stories*. Winston-Salem, NC: John F. Blair, 1978.

About the Author

A prolific travel and business writer, Bob Brooke has traveled to more than sixty-five countries, covering such diverse subjects as living under terrorism in Northern Ireland, shopping in Hong Kong, discovering the Russia of the Czars, gallery hopping in Paris, and exploring ruins in Mexico. He has authored six books, as well as articles that have appeared in many national and international publications, including *Adventure West, Delta Sky, Business Traveller, British Heritage, Discover Mexico, AntiqueWeek,* and *Executive Traveler.* He is also a regular contributor to such business publications as *The Philadelphia Business Journal* and *Operations Management,* a financial newsletter. Brooke's travel writing was given Mexico's prestigious La Pluma de Plata Award and the Real Award from Westin Hotels, and his writing on Mexico has been recognized by the National Association of Hispanic Publishers.